The Mother's Calling

LOVE IN THE HEART OF THE WORLD

Julie L. Paavola

Paulist Press
New York/Mahwah, NJ

Cover photo credit: Glenn Cratty/Loyola Marymount University
Cover and book design by Lynn Else

Library of Congress Cataloging-in-Publication Data

Paavola, Julie L.
    The mother's calling : love in the heart of the world / Julie L. Paavola.
        p. cm.
    Includes bibliographical references (p.   ).
    ISBN 978-0-8091-4701-4 (alk. paper)
    1. Mothers—Religious life. 2. Vocation—Catholic Church. 3. Motherhood—Religious aspects—Catholic Church. I. Title.
    BX2353.P23 2011
    248.8'431—dc22

                                                                    2010038014

Published by Paulist Press
997 Macarthur Boulevard
Mahwah, New Jersey 07430

www.paulistpress.com

Printed and bound in the
United States of America

Contents

For my mother,
Ardelle

Introduction

Thérèse of Lisieux was a French contemplative nun. In her autobiography, Thérèse writes how she struggled to understand her vocation in the Church, given that her entire life would be spent within the walls of a cloister. One day, as she was reading St. Paul, she understood: her calling was to be love in the heart of the Church. St. Paul had described the Church as a body, and the intensity of contemplative love was like the lifeblood of that body. It fueled the apostolic work of the Church.

A mother has a similar calling: *to be love in the heart of the world*.

It is a mother's work to honor the sacredness of the earth and of each new life given by God, and to keep believing in the goodness of creation for the sake of generations to come.

CHAPTER ONE
You Are Chosen
The Mother's Calling

Jesus answered her, "If you knew the gift of God, and who
it is that is saying to you, 'Give me a drink,' you would have
asked him, and he would have given you living water."

John 4:10

Throughout history and around the globe, there is no calling so
ubiquitous as motherhood. It is as common as our daily bread.
And yet, when a woman becomes a mother for the first time,
suddenly something so routine and mundane becomes an explo-
sive power in her life. It is as if she were on a plane bound for
Cincinnati and the plane's captain comes on the loudspeaker and
announces the flight is headed for Thailand. Her direction simply changes. And while she may have planned for years to have
a child, it is impossible to really understand the repercussions of
that decision until it becomes a reality in her own life. For as
with many things, going through an experience personally gives
us that inside view. We comprehend its meaning in our very bodies and not just intellectually or abstractly. A car crash, the death
of beloved parent, an illness, a lottery prize, a first smash hit
song, the purchase of a first house, or military enlistment and an
overseas tour of duty—all these are only conceptual until we
jump in with both feet and swim in the water of experience.

Over the years we naturally grow accustomed to being
mothers. We may even become blasé and forgetful of the importance of the mother-work we do. Yet motherhood originates in

God. It is constant throughout our lives. Other aspects of our work and interests may come and go, but no matter where we live or what new things we learn to do, something deep within us changes irrevocably when we become mothers, which cannot be lost or taken away. It is this mysterious change in us that *The Mother's Calling* wishes to explore.

THE GIFT OF GOD

In the gospel story of the Woman at the Well, Jesus asks a Samaritan woman for a drink (John 4:7). She has a bucket, access to water, and the strength to draw some of it for Jesus: the Lord asks her to perform a task within her reach. Jesus' request is an insight into the dynamic at play when a person answers God's calling. We are like the Samaritan woman sitting by her well. In summoning each of us to a particular task, career, or way of life, God asks us for a drink of water. He tailors the request he makes of us to a task within our reach. Our work, interests, passions, hopes, and dreams are firmly rooted in who we are, and the request God makes leads us, although by sometimes unusual, challenging, or even difficult pathways toward growing fidelity to that deepest identity. Our own passions are a clue of the direction God is calling each of us.

Jesus goes beyond the initial request for water and invites the Samaritan woman to *know* who is speaking to her. He identifies himself as the source of "living water." All that we can give in response to our calling, Jesus rewards with a far greater gift. He offers intimate friendship with himself and an invitation into the family of God. The calling and our response are rooted in God's own desire for intimacy, friendship, and love with his people. Jesus is asking us: give me what you have, what is at hand, and what is within reach—your daily tasks, whether important or small, hidden or public, amazing or mundane— and I will give you myself, my friendship, and all that I have. The words of the prophet Isaiah come to mind:

Everyone who thirsts,
    come to the waters;
and you that have no money,
    come, buy and eat!
Come buy wine and milk
    without money and without price.
Why do you spend your money for that which is not
        bread,
    and your labor for that which does not satisfy?
Listen carefully to me, and eat what is good,
    and delight yourselves in rich food. (Isa 55:1–2)

God calls all people in order to give each one this living water.[1]

The most basic characteristic of God's calling is its gratuitousness. It is a gift. The invitation to accept and live out this gift requires love in action, through the specific and concrete embodiment (incarnation) of God's will for us. Seeing this and taking it to heart allows us to respond in freedom and with growing joy. We do not have to be cynical, suspicious, and fearful of God's intentions or of the eventual repercussions of our affirmative answer. We can even grow in the desire to spend our energy confronting the obstacles that get in the way of living our calling to the utmost. But the really good news is that happiness is hidden in giving ourselves wholly to our unique calling. When we are frequently tempted to compare ourselves to other people, we often feel like we never do enough. At one time or another, we all feel this inadequacy. But God's infinite wisdom has appointed a time and place for each of us, a mission that is ours and ours alone. In a mysterious exchange between God's love and our individual free choice, we have the power to be a completely unique force in the universe to further the plan of God. This indeed is a gift!

MOTHERHOOD

Motherhood is notoriously an initiation through trial by fire. As Ellyn Sanna remarks, it is "the end of what has gone before."[2] Perhaps the reason becoming a mother can be so fraught with difficulty is that the challenge to our identity is both unexpected and out of sync with what society tells us about how to live our lives. Motherhood, says popular culture, is just one aspect of "having it all." Yet once we experience motherhood personally, we realize it could never merely be an "accessory." It is not even the whole outfit. It is the very skin under the outfit. It is, as Sanna rightly points out, a transformative experience, signifying the death of a part of our very selves and the birth of something new. It is only natural to resist letting go of our former identity and way of life, but it is the one way we grow into this amazing new experience called motherhood.[3]

There is also no one monolithic experience for women when they cross the threshold into motherhood. Mothers are young and middle-aged; single, married, divorced, widowed; they work inside the home or at paid jobs; they are poor, middle-class, or rich; celebrities or unknowns.

However, in the midst of this multiplicity of experience, there is also unity: birth, like death, which is often called the great equalizer, is universal. Mothers all share the wonder, delight, and pride as they look at their child for the first time. They also share certain feelings of worry or anxiety, a desire to protect their child and help it thrive. One thing is certain: the birth of a child is a moving experience that deeply touches mothers.

Sometimes, mothers can find themselves lost in the particulars of juggling work and family as they struggle to attend to their children and their own personal needs. Activity seems to rule a mother's life and one can be hopelessly caught up in details and tasks. The universals are powerful though, and we all have glimpses of it. I remember one day being intensely frustrated as I was attempting to get the attention of my three-year-old. He was ignoring me entirely. Finally, I bent down and looked him in the eyes, but saying nothing. He stopped. When he smiled at me, I was surprised at how looking at him, giving him my attention, changed the whole dynamic. I relaxed a little and my gaze made him glad. We had a split second of silent happiness because the many particulars on my agenda gave way to the universal—his littleness, which God affirmed was good, as was true of all creation (Gen 1). Paying attention allowed me to experience the universal. But I had to stop for a minute.

The archaic meaning of *attention* is "to wait," as born out by the modern French verb for *wait*—*atendre*—which has the same root. The Latin *attendere* means "to bend to." Waiting and bending: what mothers do all the time. Mothers can miss so many small treasures, however, and while they still need to get things done in a day, they will enjoy their day more and show love more consistently if they wait, slow down, and bend down to pay attention. *Pay* is also a good word because it is an investment in a lifelong relationship with our child each time we take time to look into their eyes, help them with their own small things, and encourage them with our patience. These attitudes can be very difficult to practice, and many of us need to train ourselves to slow down. But I believe our children and our spouses will notice these efforts. It is often a hands-off style, rather than a controlling, helicopter-mom style, a heart attentiveness that can give us a window into the universal.

It can be troublesome to speak of universals. Many of us obsess with historicity, particularity, and the here and now. Universals are actually rooted in the concrete particulars of life; they point to shared experiences that emphasize our commonalities. Acknowledging some kind of universals helps us understand that human beings perceive the world around us in similar ways. We all experience the helplessness of a newborn child, the beauty of nature, the comfort of human love. We are interrelated and mutually dependent like a complex ecosystem, not small, individual islands. Modern life can dull our sense of connectedness on this perceiving-and-feeling level as we are confronted with instant communication, endless information, and overwhelming pressure to go on to the next activity.

Universals help us get at what is most important about the calling of motherhood, which is not which hospital your child is born in or what kind of birth announcements you have. The moment a father holds his baby for the first time; the moment a mother first feels love for that child, usually before he or she is even born; the moment you sense deep within your heart that you would give your life for that child in a heartbeat—these are the moments we hold on to. We behold beauty firsthand. Our children give us small tastes of the beauty of God and the creation God has given to us. We also feel goodness and truth in these first parenting moments: the goodness of this particular child, who is half each from mother and father, the goodness of the mysterious code we call genetics. We taste the goodness of creation as we look at our child in amazement. The truth of the value of every human life began for each of us in this helpless form. These are concepts, of course, but more important they are key human experiences. Without them, we could all agree that our quality of life would be down around zero.

Sometimes parents of special needs children are more in touch with these universals than the rest of us. They notice beauty is bigger than a perfectly formed body and goodness is deeper than perfect health. Forced to pay attention (to wait and to bend) to the physical and emotional needs of their children in a sustained way, these parents are in a position to notice what we can too easily forget as our children grow older and become more independent.

VOCATION: ANSWERING THE CALL

New parents quickly leave the sanctuary of the delivery room and find themselves smack dab in the middle of a financial discernment process. One working parent (too often presumed to be the woman) may have to scale back or quit a job; a childcare provider may be required. Both may even be necessary. Obviously, caring for a child requires time and resources, but because housing and other costs have mandated households with two wage earners, the work vs. family dilemma is especially acute. Some families cannot afford to quit paid work, while others cannot afford to keep two incomes if childcare, commuting, and other costs related to holding down a job make it more economical for one person to stay home. Besides these financial considerations, many women enjoy their work and do not wish to abandon their careers. Work and family have to be put together somehow. Doing this has become a complicated puzzle, involving not only financial necessity and time limitations, but also the all-important question of identity and vocation. When a woman shifts her career to part time or changes it in response to having a child, she must negotiate a further identity shift over and above the transition to motherhood.

The word *vocation* is often used in the context of work or a chosen career. What does a vocation mean and how does it contrast with calling? Identity is largely rooted in the work we do, how we spend our time each day, and how our talents are put to use in a specific way of life or profession. "What do you do for living?" is another way of saying, "Who are you?" In Catholic tradition, vocation is a descriptor for men and women who have entered the religious life or the clergy. Referring to religious or clerical life as a "vocation" reflects the fact that only God can prompt them to choose this way of life. The etymology of the word is related to the Spanish *voz*, which means "voice," and the Latin *vocare*, whose root is also "voice."

As a writer, I like the metaphor of "voice" that is inherent in the word *vocation*. Each of us has a "sound" to make during our lifetimes, a song or a message, a mark to leave. Our individuality brings urgency to an intuitive conviction that living according to our individual inclinations and talents will enable us to do that one thing that will make a difference in the world. This kind of energy is most noticeable in young people, for they possess a sense of wonder at the possibilities before them. Idealism and a certain naiveté allow them to think big and to sustain hope, which can enable them to fulfill their dreams. They often have the desire to do some good in the world and not simply seek their own success. This points to the natural link between individual voice and the community in which each of us is formed. Despite the individuality and uniqueness at work in vocation, it is that very particularity that places each of us in dialogue with others and locates us within a given community. Somehow, living out the talents we were born with and nurturing them to do something good in the world are a dynamic response to specific needs around us. A bird glorifies the Creator through flight, but a person vocalizes who he or she is in the presence of fellow human beings, taking action and thereby praising God.

No wonder there is a correlation between people's satisfaction at work (all things being equal) and their overall happiness! And no wonder there is a drive toward fulfillment. It is by contributing something of who we are to the world we live in that we express our very humanity.

When considering calling and vocation in the context of motherhood, it helps to contrast the two. Calling refers to who we are. The Hebrew idiom for *calling* (*qara'*) suggests the creative act of God: "God called the light Day and the darkness he called Night" (Gen 1:5a). This shows us that, when God speaks, he creates. When he calls us, we become what his word indicates. The image of Michelangelo's creation scene on the ceiling of the Sistine Chapel comes to mind. The Father points (indicates) and, out of the tip of his finger, Adam comes into being, a metaphor for how God creates each of us intentionally. The word and the gesture demonstrate God's choice to create. That calling is given to each one individually. Not only that, but this summons from God's initiative is irrevocable (Rom 11:29). It cannot be unsaid. Calling refers to God's initiative to begin the conversation, a conversation made up of actions, not only words. God calls us in fundamental ways: into existence, to a particular time and place, to faith, to listen to the Word of God, to know him, and to become associated with the family of God.

By contrast, let us look at vocation as our response to God's initiative. We might say vocation is what we do with God's call or summons. Our response to God is commonly multivocal. It is not necessarily a "singular pursuit: one person, one gender, one vocation."[4] Throughout our lives we respond to our very existence, glorifying God, giving thanks for the gift of life, depending on our individual gifts and our particular history.[5] What we do in life is our response to God's calling; our vocation refers to our intentionality about that response. It is our voiced expression in a dynamic exchange between Creator and creature that expresses God's fidelity and our need to make something of our one, unique life.

Becoming a mother can intensify a woman's sense of vocation, for she must decide what to embrace and what to let go of. "Prioritizing" is a poor term for what really involves a deep pruning away of all that is superfluous so that she may own her truest identity. As she makes difficult choices and sorts out what is most important, she grows in self-knowledge. Motherhood can put in perspective the importance of holding on to what is most truly expressive of our unique calling in life and impels us to efficiently clean house of all that is not essential. Some women even experience a revival of their creative powers when they start a family. Rather than negating the threads of vocation that express who we are, having a child can be an opportunity for us to own them more forcefully. The greatest freedom possible should be given to encourage women to make positive decisions for themselves and their families so that they can answer the call to motherhood while honoring other aspects of their vocation.

MAKING SOMETHING OF OUR LIVES

One of the greatest mothers in Scripture is Sarah, whose story is told in Genesis. Just as Abraham is called by tradition "our father in faith," so Sarah is our mother in faith, because she was specifically selected to give birth to the Chosen People, Israel. Her road to motherhood is a rocky one. During her many travels with Abraham, Sarah shares in his trials and the sheer adventure of obedience to God. She too leaves her father's house for a new land, accepts the Lord as her own God, and places her hope in his promises. The greatest promise of all those that God makes to Abraham is the promise that he will be the father of a great nation (Gen 12:2). Over the years that Abraham and Sarah look for the fulfillment of this promise, Sarah remains barren, and so Abraham chooses Eliezer his servant as his heir. Sarah also takes matters into her own hands and sends her slave girl Hagar to become her husband's concubine and produce an heir. This slave girl bears a child to Abraham, Ishmael. But the Lord insists that neither Eliezer nor Ishmael will inherit what he has promised Abraham (Gen 15:3–4; 17:15–16). God chooses Sarah herself to be the mother of Israel, and in every passage where God reiterates the promise to Abraham, Sarah is also either implied or explicitly named. In the most obvious passage, God declares: "As for Sarai your wife, you shall not call her Sarai, but Sarah shall be her name. I will bless her and moreover I will give you a son by her. I will bless her, and she shall give rise to nations; kings of peoples shall come from her" (Gen 17:16).

God gives Sarai the name "Sarah," showing the identity shift from woman to mother—despite the fact that she is ninety years old. Abraham laughs at the idea of her pregnancy and even tries to correct the Lord on this matter (Gen 17:17–18). The new name points to her new identity, not by casting away her former self, but by adding a new dimension through God's blessing and gift. More will be given her through her mothering experience and the process of bringing up her child in God's presence, but she will never again be Sarai.

As no other experience before or since, Sarah's pregnancy and the birth of Isaac enables her faith to flower. Years of hardship and waiting have tried her faith, but now God's promise has been actualized in her very body.

Waiting and hoping for something for many years can cause our inner resources to fail us. We begin to loose that exuberance of joy we had in our youth, when a dream we held dear motivated us forward to the next new challenge. Hope slips away. Sarah may well have been at a very low ebb when she overhears her husband's conversation with the three visitors who brought God's promise to the couple: "I shall surely return to you in due season, and your wife Sarah shall have a son" (Gen 18:10). She laughs to herself because she is old, her husband is old, and finding "pleasure" seems ludicrous to her. Had she lost pleasure in life in general? Perhaps there is some bitterness and even sorrow in her laughter. It seems too late for her. Her light is going out, and her path ending. God's promises are a fading mirage, seeming to hold only dry dust and disappointment. Yet the way God deals with Sarah, and the way he fulfills the great promise he made to her, teaches her to recognize his power: her barrenness and old age are not obstacles to him.

It must have been the greatest shock of her life when the old words she heard over and over again finally came to pass. Sarah was with child! During the days of her pregnancy, Sarah must have pondered in her heart—as Mary, the mother of Jesus, would ponder generations later—the promise and action of God and its meaning in her life: nothing is too wonderful or impossible for God, and all generations would call her blessed, for God has done great things for her (cf. Gen 18:14a and Luke 1:36–38). God could even give Sarah a child out of her aging body. Through and in her weakness, God forced an "encounter with the divine." As Bonnie J. Miller-McLemore writes, ordinary family life is a place for faith and a primary instance of encounter with the divine for mothers, as it was for Sarah.[6] While Abraham had seven encounters with God, recorded as conversations, Sarah's covenant with God is expressed in the very events of her life, where God is involved by acting in her favor, blessing her, and urging her with the powerful Spirit. God was plotting his covenant with Abraham while he was knitting the embodiment of the covenant in the womb of Sarah.

Abraham and Sarah: conversation in prayer and embodiment in action. Abraham symbolizes our solitude, when we seek the Father in private (see Matt 6:6). Sarah symbolizes our continuous offering of our lives to God "as a living sacrifice," which is how she showed her willingness to be part of God's design for humanity's salvation. St. Paul calls this willingness "holy and acceptable to God" (Rom 12:1–3). The encounter with the divine takes place in prayer and in life, and they reflect each other. Together, faith and work bear out the reality of God in the concrete world to express an embodied spirituality.

When Isaac is born, Sarah laughs. I imagine an expressive, guttural sound, like the deep bellows of labor, voicing the depths of her transformation. This laugh is entirely different from the titter she gave after overhearing the three visitors. She sees the irony. God has chided her and cajoled her. She has looked away, pointed to someone else, ranted, and spat on the ground. But today, her laughter is pure. Bitterness and regret have dissolved. Her very child is named Isaac, *laughter*, for God has triumphed in her and he is great enough to absorb her pain and fill her with thanksgiving. "God has brought laughter for me; everyone who hears will laugh with me" (Gen 21:6).

God chooses us and visits us as he did Sarah. Giving us the gift of a child, God invites us to laugh with Sarah, to recognize the very hand of God in each of our children. Even if we conceived easily, it is no less God's miracle, God's child. We are stewards and participants in something far-reaching: God's own project of creation and salvation. We laugh when our minds expect one thing and another comes to pass. Just so, God works by surprising us, flipping us on our heads, giving us more than we could hope for and other than we had planned: not on our timeline but his, not on our planned route but his, which always involves transformation and conversion along the way.

MOTHERHOOD TODAY

It is striking how the gospels portray Jesus reaching out to tax collectors and sinners and the resulting criticism from the religious authorities. Jesus told his detractors in clear, simple language to stop judging. This is a wonderful starting place for mothers. There are as many ways to be a mother as there are to be a human being. Mothers have babies. We also adopt. We care for grandchildren and for friends' children. We are single mothers or married. We may become widowed or divorced. Some work long hours at jobs we'd quit in a heartbeat if we had the choice. Others work hard within a chosen career we love. We love our kids and we struggle to love them better. We all fail in one way or another. We would probably fail a lot less, or at least get through our failures with more grace, if we judged each other less and supported each other more—no matter what our particular incarnation of motherhood. Perhaps the reason for the so-called mommy wars and the judgmental attitudes that seem to accompany them is rooted not in our diverse choices as mothers, but in societal expectations of women, the expectation of perfection.

Parents today are plagued by fear of failure. With so many options available to us for the benefit of our children in terms of comfort, safety, health, education, and entertainment, many of us feel responsible for every facet of our children's lives and suffer enormous guilt if something goes wrong. Exposure to "choice overload" can pressure us to make the *right* choices and achieve maximum benefit. We may even subconsciously be aiming not only for perfection in terms of which choices we make, but our children as perfect outcomes. When we expect perfection, from ourselves or from our kids, everyone is disappointed. Besides this, we may miss the glory of simple pleasures and the satisfaction of our many small successes. The sunset is there, but we don't see it because we are too busy completing our busy schedules, aiming for perfection.

Women bear the brunt of the fear of failing as parents. That old myth that women develop an angelic nature after becoming mothers only intensifies the perfection myth. On the contrary, as Anne Tremaine Linthorst writes, "Sometimes children provoke our worst selves rather than our best selves."[7] Any parent who is a stay-at-home mom or dad knows the truth of these words. There is little in our formation or upbringing to prepare us for dealing with weaknesses and failure. Many of us go from success to success in our adult lives—we graduate from college, get jobs, earn money, enjoy hobbies, and make friends. We derive a sense of satisfaction from our accomplishments and feel that we are good people. We achieve a sense of control and equilibrium. Freedom to travel and to come and go easily enables many of us to feel we have a lot of say over our time and the way our life is progressing.

Suddenly this tiny infant comes into our lives. This brand new human being reintroduces us to life's messiness and unpredictability. Our freedom to come and go is halted or slowed down. Nursing, changing diapers, washing clothes, transforming our homes into safe zones, comforting and coaxing, visiting doctors, finding playtime, and being patient at cry time—all this rules our lives. We feel like servants and our former "success" seems to fade away into the background like a forgotten dream.

All of this undermines our sense of control and balance. It messes with our self-image and deals a blow to our egos. A myriad of hot-button issues shakes up our world, and everything comes down in a different place: our job, relationships with friends and family, marriage, hobbies, exercise, even prayer. Negotiating this shake up tests our self-esteem as it makes us worry about failure.

The weakness we feel when we face a transition or a difficult challenge has a special purpose in our spiritual growth. Through it, God can work within us a growing trust in him and a greater capacity for loving others. Our moment of weakness becomes a remarkable opportunity. In the Christian understanding, spirituality is always a process of transformation, not simply a discovery. God is still at work in us: we are God's work of art and, as of yet, incomplete. This transformation has one goal, to form us in the image of Christ as children of God. Far from being an impediment, our weakness drives us toward God, who enables us to become more fully human, thus more capable of doing great good.

Failure is part of what it means to be human. One writer even claims that, because of failure, "we achieve our true identities."[8] Our routine failures probably won't harm our kids, although our anxiety about them might. As with any great adventure, transformation requires commitment and sacrifice. The commitment and sacrifice required as we launch out into parenthood present the opportunity to practice what Christianity traditionally calls asceticism. Asceticism happens on two levels, one active and one passive.

On the active level, a mother enters a discipline of giving that requires an enormous amount of energy. She gives birth, and she may nurse her child; she serves it out of the strength of her own body. Putting herself in a secondary place in favor of another requires renunciation. Yet even as she embraces the demands of parenthood, she is touched by a certain freedom that comes from this dedication. She, her husband, and others who care for the child leave behind some of their self-centeredness and take part in God's ways and God's thoughts, which are far above our own (Isa 55:9), loving completely this child whom God called before he or she was born, and named while he or she was still in the womb (Isa 49:1). Only God can enable us to love this way, with this unconditional love.

Naming and calling are, once again, synonymous ways of speaking of what God does for us. God loves us into existence and promises that our existence is not futile. As we welcome a child into the world, we participate in the creative, unconditional Creator-Love of God. We name our child, a symbolic participation in the very creative act of God. By countless, deliberate choices and efforts we make for our children, we act to further God's desire for each one, even as God "plans for your welfare…to give you a future with hope" (Jer 29:11). While God formed this child in the womb to prepare it for this life, parents form the child in this life in order to prepare it for the next.

There is another side to this asceticism that is just as all-encompassing: the unexpected. Passive asceticism refers to what life and circumstances throw at us, late-night emergency-room visits, serious illnesses, troubles with discipline or in school, the painful decisions grown children make that we may not agree with. Our heart's desire is to give our children the very best upbringing possible and to protect them. Paradoxically, we ourselves must deal with each new challenge knowing we are often not up to the job, improvising. When the unexpected happens, and it is often something we cannot easily avoid, we go forward and do our best. These ordeals break open our hearts in ways we never imagined. They teach us something about ourselves and also about our children. While we naturally struggle against this kind of passive asceticism, it is the cost of love and the gateway to the kind of freedom that comes with loving unselfishly.

In our time and place, culture insists that we can have it all. This message hides a secret falsehood: it pretends that we can love without sacrifice. Parenting involves both active and passive asceticism for the sake of loving our children unconditionally, which does involve sacrifice. Furthermore, we can love this way with the help of grace. Human love that is selfless participates in divine love, whether we know it or not, whether we are believers or not. God promotes this love in any willing human heart, building on our natural desire to love and be loved, carrying us above our limited capacity to love as God does. This is the special gift a woman participates in through mothering. The father also shares this gift, but she receives it first and shares her firsthand knowledge of the initial sacrifices required of her in pregnancy and birth. She introduces the father to the gift of love that both parents are summoned by God to give their child.

This kind of love does not require perfection. It can even exist in the most imperfect of parents. Ellyn Sanna reminds us that even if we could be perfect, it would not be desirable. Our children would then "remain needy and dependent" and never separate from us.[9] On the other hand, if children learn that fallibility is normal, they will not unrealistically demand perfection of themselves. When my two boys were still quite young, I discovered the power of a humble apology for my own obvious misdeeds. I'd find a quiet time at the end of the day, usually at bedtime prayers, to tell my four-year-old and my seven-year-old I was sorry when I lost control, yelled at them, or complained. Sometime we parents are exhausted and worn down; we feel totally justified in losing it. However, when we lack discipline in ourselves, we cannot effectively discipline our kids. When anger and selfishness are in the driver's seat, our children know it before we do. There is no point in pretending it isn't so. Sanna reminds us, "Our mistakes can be infused with God's grace."[10] Grace is the key, for it comes to our assistance powerfully when we acknowledge our limitations and do not lord it over our children. Can we be humble with them?

Motherhood calls us to set aside our judgmental attitudes—with ourselves, with other women who walk this path, and with our children. If we can walk this path in humility and with frank realism, we can enjoy more of life. We can worry less and love more naturally.

ENCOUNTER AND PRACTICE

Encounter

Read the story of the Woman at the Well in John 4. Here Jesus has a conversation with a regular woman as she goes about her chores. This conversation is prayer, which St. Teresa of Avila called a conversation between two friends. Sit down by your own "well," a place where you feel quiet or at rest, in nature, alone in your room, anywhere that works for you. Imagine Jesus close-by. He sits down with us at the well of our daily reality and greets us where we are:

1. Share with him where you are today in terms of your feelings.
2. See in your mind or heart that Jesus is asking you, "Give me a drink." What is your offering today, something within reach that expresses something of God's calling to you and your own response, your voice, your song to God?
3. Hear Jesus offer you his "living water." Water connotes desire and the need to satisfy our longings. What does "living water" mean to you at this time in your life? How do you hope Christ will quench your thirsts?

Practice

Bonnie Miller-McLemore wrote that the purpose of her book was "to share a sense of the grace that can come when we are honest about the difficulties and attentive to the blessings present in everyday life."[11] What follows are a few suggestions for inviting God's grace into our lives.

1. *Bend and Wait.* Take the time today to practice looking into your child's eyes. You can do this when you first greet him or her after school or play. You can even try it when he or she is upset or naughty. Bend down. Get his attention and focus your attention on his face, especially the eyes. Usually this quiets both of you down if there is a ruckus going on. In that small window of a shared look, notice what transpires. Open your heart to what God is speaking to you about your child and your relationship. Exchange a word or two if you

want. This can be a word of greeting or praise, something positive. Practice this a few times a day.

2. *Bear Patiently.* We have our first child before we have the time to adjust to being a mother. As we grow into our identity as mothers, we may run into problems if we believe we must be perfect.[12] Patience with ourselves teaches us how to practice it with our children. The word *patience* comes from *pati*, which means to "undergo, suffer, or bear."[13] Take some time to examine your conscience. How much perfection do you demand of yourself? Do you routinely feel you are not meeting your own or others' expectations? Put your list down for a moment and ask, What does God wish for me today? If you do what is right in front of you, you are already doing what pleases God. Each piece of clothing you fold, each phone call you make, each client you interact with—every task you do is enough.

CHAPTER TWO

Be Fruitful and Multiply

A Spirituality of Pregnancy and Childbirth

> The angel said to her, "Do not be afraid, Mary, for you have found favor with God. And now, you will conceive in your womb and bear a son, and you will name him Jesus."
>
> Luke 1:30–31

God placed the world's salvation in the hands of a teenage girl from Palestine. In an astonishing gesture of trust, God opened a dialogue with Mary of Nazareth and offered her, not a promise, but the Promised One in flesh and blood—Jeshua, which means "God saves." What an enormous responsibility!

Mary's story has a uniqueness that is unparalleled because she became the mother of Jesus, but her story does not end there. Like a heavenly traveler through time, Mary is involved with *our* lives. Jewish mother that she is, she guides us so we too may find favor with God and learn to find joy in the Lord above all else: "My soul magnifies the Lord and my spirit rejoices in God my savior" (Luke 1:46–47). Her story and her presence are especially poignant for women who are struggling to understand their calling in today's world. We will take Mary as our companion as we look at pregnancy and childbirth as central aspects of our lives and so a key part of our faith journey.

PREGNANCY AS HOPE AND DESIRE

Pregnancy is a time of waiting, hoping, and preparing. It is an immersion in Motherhood 101, a crash course in learning to consider the needs of another human being uninterruptedly. Everything we do, say, eat—even how we sleep and what we secretly feel—are suddenly shared with another human being. Decisions we deemed highly personal are now no longer ours alone, as we sort out how best to nurture a healthy pregnancy. Most of all, there is a growing and overwhelming expectation, a kind of incredulous wonder at this someone who is coming, a child who will forever change the landscape of our life. Who and what that someone will be is already in motion and yet we know so little. We sit in metaphoric darkness even as the baby forming in our womb sits in actual darkness. During these crucial months, our waiting will be active and deliberate. We will attend classes, ask opinions, take vitamins, talk to our friends, deliberate with our husbands, paint rooms, and avoid painkillers. Sooner or later we will start to buy tiny pieces of clothing and stare in wonder, trying to imagine how a live human being could actually fit inside. Sometimes we'll daydream. Sometimes we'll feel our pregnant bellies and wonder. Sometimes we'll weep. Through all this, our desire grows as we picture holding our child for the first time.

Imagine Mary's pregnancy. We have no way of knowing how she took care of herself during pregnancy, but we do have some idea of what her life was like during those nine months. She was to marry Joseph. Along with her people, Mary must have prayed for the Messiah. Yet when she became pregnant, she was still on her own. Mary doesn't try to solve this question herself. Instead, she spends the first trimester of her pregnancy with Elizabeth, assisting her with her own pregnancy and birth. It is significant that Mary leaves her solitude and immediately goes to help Elizabeth. This may not have been her first time helping with childbirth, but now she herself is a mother, and both she and Elizabeth know that their pregnancies are part of God's work being done in them. As Elizabeth says to her when Mary first arrives, "As soon as I heard the sound of your greeting, the child in my womb leaped for joy. And blessed is she who believed that there would be a fulfillment of what was spoken to her by the Lord" (Luke 1:44–45). These two pregnant women are the first to know that the centuries of waiting are over and that the promise to Abraham and Sarah is being fulfilled now, in them.

When Mary returns, she must face the brokenhearted Joseph, who as yet does not understand what is happening. Joseph has just determined to divorce Mary quietly instead of "exposing her to public disgrace" when the Lord sends an angel to him with the instruction, "Joseph, son of David, do not be afraid to take Mary as your wife, for the child conceived in her is from the Holy Spirit" (Matt 1:19–20). When things finally settle down and Joseph takes her as his wife, Mary is on the move again. The couple must go to Bethlehem to register in the census during the remaining weeks of her final trimester. She has no luxury to sit alone and contemplate. She must have clung to the words, "nothing shall be impossible with God," the words also spoken to Sarah, the first mother in Jesus' lineage (Gen 18:14; Luke 1:37).

Through all the joy of being with Elizabeth and the turmoil of feeling Joseph's uncertainty, Mary continues to ponder her pregnancy as a fulfillment of centuries of hope. She is coming to understand some of the things that are happening to her. When she had asked, "How can this be, since I am a virgin?" (Luke 1:34), Gabriel responded with a fourfold answer: It can be through the Holy Spirit. It can be because of the identity of the child, Son of God. It can be because Elizabeth her kinswoman is with child, and Mary is not alone in her God-appointed task. It can be because nothing is impossible with God (Luke 1:35–38). Mary already holds the Desired One, Christ, within her body. Her way of coping with the reality of her pregnancy is to ponder (Luke 1:29, 2:19, 2:51). As she ponders, her hope turns to desire as fulfillment nears.

Sanna and others have said pregnancy has a way of mending the artificial split between body and spirit.[1] In her own pregnancy, Mary must have felt complete unity between her spiritual longing and her bodily readiness as the time drew near. Her Lord had gone within, and she worshiped by going down, not up—down into the mystery of a God who had descended into her womb in order to bring her and all people up to the Father (John 10:28–30). Every embodied person, through Mary's desire for God, is free to become God's new temple. There can be no question from this point forward about the sacredness of our physical bodies. All humanity is made holy, made righteous or right with God, through this coming of God into a human body. What happened in Mary continues in us through our own spiritual journey.

The season of Advent is dedicated to Mary's pregnancy and coincides with our own hope-filled expectation of God's coming. As people of faith, we now take on the expectancy of the pregnant Mary. It is not passive waiting, but tiptoe expectancy. In the language of Christian faith, it is directly linked with desire. This desire is a longing of the heart, of which Augustine has spoken of so eloquently in his *Confessions*: "You have made us for yourself and our hearts find no peace until they rest in you."[2] The O Antiphons, sung since the time of the early Church during the week preceding Christmas, both describe and feed this desire:

> O Wisdom, O holy Word of God,...come and show your people the way to salvation....O sacred Lord of Ancient Israel, who showed yourself to Moses in the burning bush, who gave him the holy law on Sinai mountain: come, stretch out your mighty hand to set us free....O Flower of Jesse's stem,...the nations bow down in worship before you. Come, let nothing keep you from coming to our aid....O Key of David,...come, break down the prison walls of death...and lead your captive people into freedom. O Radiant Dawn, splendor of eternal light, sun of justice: come, shine on those who dwell in darkness....O King of all the nations, the only joy of every human heart,...come and save the creature you fashioned

from the dust...O Emmanuel, king and lawgiver, desire of the nations, Savior of all People, come and set us free, Lord our God."[3]

Desire is the lifeblood of the spiritual life. As blood in our veins brings life to all the parts of our body, so desire shapes the trajectory of our lives God-ward. We long for freedom, happiness, knowledge, truth, peace, prosperity, and beauty. As we seek these things, our hidden need for God emerges, for he alone can consummate such desires. He does not purge us of longings in order to supplant them with some divine agenda for our good that has nothing to do with us. God seeds desire in our hearts so that he may direct our footsteps and help us work toward the fulfilled life that only he can work in us. St. Ignatius speaks of this desire in his Spiritual Exercises, a guidebook for those who would direct others on retreat and in prayer. He believed it was so important to keep desire at the forefront of the spiritual life that he placed this instruction at the beginning of every period of prayer: "I will make known to God our Lord that which I want and desire."[4]

When Mary heard the words of the angel who greeted her, she was already pregnant with desire for God. Her hope led to desire. Her desire led to action: "Here am I, the servant of the Lord; let it be with me according to your word" (Luke 1:38). Nowhere was there anyone else so entirely at one with God's desire to give the world a Savior! Through the purity of her desire for the Messiah, Mary conceived Christ and out of that same longing and love she bore him. The inspiration of her virginity is not a message for us about physical purity, but an unmistakable sign of this single-hearted desire for God. The real miracle is that one person's desire could be so entirely focused on God that God became flesh in her womb.

How often do mothers think about the fact that a mother's love brought God to earth? Our love brings God to earth too. Being a mother brings God to earth when we enter into this simple hope and desire for a child. As with Mary, our hope and desire lead to action, a sustained love for our children that only just begins in our child's infancy. This love is an unbroken dedication. This sustained character of our love for our children, although we certainly do this imperfectly, unites us to God in his goodness and love as Creator. Every mother is one with the will of the Creator in a new way in pregnancy and birth, and in caring for her children over a lifetime. God's work is always going on, but it goes on through us, through people, not by divine fiat. And it goes on in ordinary human life, in families, at the workplace, during holidays, and in the routine of life in the home.

Mary helps us look at creation as something intrinsic, happening within us, not only outside of us. For the remainder of this chapter, pregnancy and birth will be viewed in the context of God's work in creation.

PREGNANCY: A SHARE IN CREATIVE LOVE

Pregnancy is a front-row seat in the splendid opera of God's continuing creation. Life surges forward under our noses day and night. Pregnancy forces us to notice. In the midst of many practical preparations, our body is a teacher, whispering secrets our minds are too limited to grasp. Suddenly we begin to learn about the force of nature from the inside out, in a personal, emotional way. Whereas before we had seen the beauty of the natural world from the outside, been inspired by mountains and the glorious sun, by quiet mornings of solitude, or by the magnificence of the coursing ocean—now this grandeur also quietly surges within. It is raw nature and it is at once part of us and other-than-us. It has a life of its own and goes forward being what it will be. Mothers share in the creative work of God, intentionally and experientially, and by feeling what the body has to teach us, we know something entirely new about God as Creator.

Genesis paints a picture of the Creator as one who makes the world out of chaos. God's spirit hovers over the depths as if beholding a large mess. And the act of creating has this character of setting order in the world, separating darkness and light, water from land, night from day, and water creatures from flying creatures and from those that crawl. God further orders the cosmos with the sun and moon to rule over their respective domains. He divides the dry land into segments by four rivers.

The God of Genesis creates anew in each pregnancy, differentiating between mother and child, between one life and another. Whatever good God has done or shown me in my life now divides into two rivers of love and mercy—one toward the mother and one toward child. Genesis describes metaphorically a reality far beyond our comprehension: the unseen love that keeps all things in the created order up and moving. It is the Energy behind energy. Genesis jumpstarts the imagination, breaking open the heart to the fathomless goodness of the God who makes all things new each morning; indeed, each and every moment.

The love behind creation, or underneath it, also reveals that God creates not out of necessity but because he delights in his creation. Pregnancy gives us a share in this. We intuitively know that each pregnancy is unique, an unrepeatable person-in-waiting. A telltale trait of parents' love is this insistence on the preciousness of each child. We call it pride, the secret bias that tells us *our* children are just a little more special than anyone else on the planet. We feel the mystery of this unique person that God has created, and we share the Creator's delight. Even in the midst of fears, hardship, and unexpected difficulties, the awesome truth of our child's completely unique being is a powerful counterweight. Here we experience God in our own parental love. God's love is the antecedent to a mother and father's love, and becomes only more dedicated and unconditional as time goes by.

A spirituality of pregnancy and childbirth sets aside the culture war over how creation originated and focuses instead on the insight that God creates all things in the present. Motherhood bridges the false divide between science and spirituality. It allows us to share in something of the omnipotent love of God who sustains all created reality, from the smallest nanoparticle to the incomprehensible black hole. The Creator *holds* creation. The mother holds her child. The holding in both cases preserves the life and wellness of the one being held. While this may remind us of our innate contingency, something we may not want to focus on, what is more important is that it gives us access to the dynamic nature of all life, always in movement, never static, always growing, never still.[5] Energizing this is the all-present love of God.

The Jesuit Joseph Tetlow describes some of the insights into the theology of creation in recent years: "God creates continually; all things grow through phases and stages throughout life; human desiring has been gravely confused by sin and disorder; our desires either express what God hopes for or we have no way of connecting with what God intends for us and the universe."[6] Let us apply each of these to pregnancy.

First, pregnancy is a present-tense experience. Mothers may realize a creative power at work that is within them and yet beyond them, the power of God, who alone gives life: "For it was you who formed my inward parts: you knit me together in my mother's womb. I praise you for I am wonderfully, fearfully made" (Ps 39:13–14a). What is happening within the womb feels like the knitting referred to in the psalm. It is a continuous happening that is astonishingly out of a mother's hands. Her prenatal vitamins and exercises are good, but the tiny cells propel forward into their complex organization without her assistance. Nature is taking its course in pregnancy, but nature itself is God's wondrous work as Genesis persistently reminds us. Here the psalmist points to a God who is immanent in nature. He gives us an image of God knitting, a surprisingly homey and feminine image, revealing the intimacy of a God who touches us, knits us—actively choosing the color of the threads of our being and the textures and shape of the garment that will be. God forms us in the smallness of our physical beginnings. Other passages show God as one who knows the whole of our lives even before we are created, as if to emphasize God's deliberate desire to bring us into being: "Before I formed you in the womb I knew you, and before you were born I consecrated you" (Jeremiah 1:5a). God calls each child into existence at a moment in time and yet knows, as only God can know, the entirety of each person's life.[7] Besides forming us in our earliest existence and knowing the whole of our lives, God gives us a name that describes who we are called to be.

While new parents often deliberate for months over the selection of a name for their child, God names us in the very act of creating. Genesis describes how God gives a name to each thing as it comes into being (Gen 1), and invites humans to share in the divine creative power by naming the animals. The name God has for each person is mysterious (Rev 3:12), for it contains both who we are and who we will be in Christ, that is when we are "finished," made perfect in Christ. The continuous nature of creation flows into the progressive aspect of growth: all things grow in stages throughout life, Tetlow's second point.

Mothers are very familiar with stages. They know their work is never done and know there is always another stage just around the corner. Pregnancy is only the beginning of a lifelong giving in love as mothers attend to their children's growth. This cannot be done alone. We share this commitment with our husband and also in the context of a community of support, knowing the "work in progress" will need many hands to continue its formation. Life is necessarily unfinished and raw; pregnancy and the parenting that necessarily follows are a face-to-face meeting with this phenomenon. This experience reminds us of our own limitations as creatures. For while God is perfect, complete, and finished, we experience every day our need for further growth. The Lord is still forming us. Many of the challenges and trials of our lives occasion our progress to the next stage of our own growth. Just as the Lord once knit us in our mothers' womb, so now he weaves us into the pattern of a child of God by drawing our hearts, our desire, to him and away from what hinders us.

Finally, motherhood is sustained giving. Family life needs a manager. Women mostly do this by focusing a large amount of their spiritual energy on their family.[8] Mothers routinely set aside their preferences and desires to care for their children. The work of nurturing requires a movement out of oneself and into the needs of another. Mothers commonly take the lead in the complex challenge of meeting the needs of children, from the details of school and home to health and recreation. Many do paid and volunteer work as well. In the friction between what we might feel like doing and what parenting calls us to, God teaches us spiritual lessons. He calls us to grow in love and emulate his love. At times, we paradoxically feel lighthearted, as when we play with a child, stopping in the midst of a busy day; or when we address their needs even though we may have many unmet needs ourselves and may not have the strength. Patience is our daily bread, a dry, hard crust on most days! But the "mother's penance" of daily life in service to our children also frees our desires God-ward. A mother's work of love is one central way God graces us as women, putting our desires through the crucible that frees us.

What does God have in mind for us, for our children, for the world, for the cosmos? God will answer our deepest desires. When our heart's desire and God's infinite love coincide, the birth of a new creation is possible.

LABOR AND BIRTH: NATURE'S GIFTS

Every expectant mother desires to one day hold her child on the other side of labor and birth. Giving birth, however, briefly transports a woman out of the habitual control normally built into our lives. Birth often involves the unplanned and the unexpected. This is an interesting place to begin our career as mothers, as if to make us ready for a whole lifetime of the unexpected. Birth educator Pam England asserts, "The profound mystery and spirituality of birth can never be understood with the mind; they are known through the heart."[9] In order to get in touch with this heart understanding, England conducts classes in which mothers-to-be and their husbands draw, paint, journal, and write poetry to discover their own innermost beliefs and feelings. "Dreams, reverie and art," she writes, "all carry messages from the unconscious."[10] Women got to know their fears and worries about labor, but were also surprised by a sense of inner strength that gave them confidence. Reflecting on the images in their drawings or on their experience after giving birth, they found they had had no idea of the richness of this hidden part of themselves.

The physiology of giving birth demands strength. In labor the body mysteriously "knows" that the time for birth has arrived, sets off a chain reaction of hormones, and initiates the process that sets labor in motion. Labor is like a triathlon in which the athlete alternates between various physical challenges in order to arrive at the finish line. The needed strength comes from within, from a mother's inner resources. At the same time, the mounting intensity of birth forces complete surrender of body and will and an opening "wide of body, mind and soul." England describes her own experience of "reaching deep inside for strength to break through the mental and physical limitations to summon all the strength possible."[11] Even in the midst of this intense, physically confrontational experience, labor also has the potential to have moments of heightened spiritual alertness. At times women have felt intense experiences in the midst of the hardest labor. Some felt at one with other women. Others were clear-headed and intensely focused on birthing. A few even thought of death near the end of labor, which surprised but didn't disturb them.[12]

Why speak of strength, alertness, or spiritual experience in the context of labor? Modern medicine enables us to avoid much if not all of the pain involved. We can simply have our babies with the help of medicine and not worry. Yet, we miss this process of self-discovery if we largely ignore our own experience around labor and birth.

I was forced into self-discovery when I was pregnant for the second time. After experiencing depression each time I went to my prenatal appointments, I realized I needed to stand up to my doctor. Labor with my first child had ended in an emergency C-section in which the intern on duty cut my son during the operation. As if that weren't enough, other mistakes were made, including a botched epidural. Now my doctor was insisting that I have another C-section, and at each visit he discouraged me from having a vaginal birth after Cesarean (VBAC). Because of my first birth experience, I knew I couldn't simply trust the professionals. As soon as I took charge of the situation, my depression left. I changed my medical group and my doctor, hired a doula to help me through labor, support me in giving birth, and advocate for me, so I could be open to natural childbirth and avoid unnecessary interference. I went into labor on the due date and gave birth with the support of my family and the medical team. Something within drove me to do this. It was that inner strength kicking in, but I never would have experienced that strength had I just followed the advice of the doctor and not listened to my heart, which had clearly spoken to me through the depression.

Women all possess strength. Birthing a child puts us in contact with our strength, allowing us to acknowledge it in the form of intense emotional and physical work. It is this capacity which helps us as mothers. It is what enables us to deal with the most difficult challenges in life and in the lives of our families. Our strength is part of our gift as women. It is not a solitary experience but one that assumes partnership. When we allow ourselves to assert this strength, paradoxically we become aware of support and companionship.

UNLIKELY COMPANIONS

Women have two unlikely companions in labor and birth, Mary and God. Mary exemplifies the support we find in other women. Mary gave birth away from home, in Bethlehem: "While they were there the time came for her to deliver her child. And she gave birth to her firstborn son, and wrapped him in bands of cloth, and laid him in a manger, because there was no place for them in the inn"(Luke 2:6–7). Most likely Mary gave birth in a cave, since they were commonly used to shelter animals. It is hard to imagine giving birth in those circumstances—on the road, with none of the comforts of home, and, worst of all, no female relatives to help her. Mary's birthing of Jesus is not described here as miraculous. Instead, Luke states her time of delivery was completed, like any other would be, and that she simply "gave birth." Did she feel at one with all the mothers through history? Did she also reach inside to draw strength? The gospel depicts Mary as someone who is surprised by birth, just as we are. Birth has a way of happening at the most inconvenient time! She had swaddling clothes, but no cradle, so she used a mother's ingenuity and opted for the manger. All of this tells us that Mary is someone we would want by our side in pregnancy and birthing. Her own circumstances would lead her to empathize with whatever unusual situations we might find ourselves in as mothers. Luke's gospel portrays Mary as a companion, a sister, or a mother who would understand our messy lives and our own challenging experiences in pregnancy and birth.

The sense of Mary as our companion is lost on many modern Christians. However, Mary's companionship is prevalent in the Hispanic community. A well-known song, *Santa Maria del Camino*, sung in Hispanic liturgies throughout the country, speaks of this: "As you go traveling this life, you are never alone. With you on the road, holy Mary goes too." And the refrain repeats, "Come with us to walk, holy Mary, come." The verses remind us that while it may seem "futile to keep walking," we are making new roads for others to follow; that although some say "nothing can change," we struggle for a new world and for the truth. Mary, in each refrain, is invited to be our companion in a life that is not easy or miraculous, but difficult and ordinary.

The emphasis in this and many other Marian songs is on faith. They remind us Mary is our fellow traveler helping us to live by faith, reminding us we are loved and not alone in our greatest difficulties. Just as it is a consolation when we are suffering to bring to mind the life of Christ, it is important, especially for women, to remember what the Mother of the Lord endured because of her decision to collaborate in the work of God, which the angel revealed and she accepted.

How is God our companion in labor and birth? Genesis describes God working with deliberation, planning the created world as it unfolds. Then, God rests on the seventh day, as if exhausted. This image of a God who is wrung out by the creative act inspires us to consider: since God could not have been literally tired, the story must point to something more. What does it mean to say that God labors or works? Taking the liberty of anthropomorphizing God for a moment, we might say God's act of creation ushers in a new "experience" for God. Human beings were made in the image of God; that is, with freedom of will and with intellect. The independent nature of each person caused a new vulnerability in the created world, because it implies the possibility to mistrust, refuse, or disobey God. Thus, the new "experience" for God was vulnerability.

In the act of birthing, mothers share in this vulnerability. Though formerly intimately bound to her, suddenly the child becomes an independent person. This is "the most dramatic of all separations," followed by a long sequence of letting go, which will take different forms as the child develops and grows up, departing in successive journeys outward and away.[13] So crucial is this letting go that our children can live and grow only if we do this. It is simply integral to human development. The whole instinct of mothering is to protect and nurture, yet the actual work of mothering is a back and forth between embracing and letting go, between keeping within the sanctuary of home and sending off to school, between dependence and independence. This back and forth of giving and letting go emulates the free gift of the Creator's love. For God also simultaneously keeps us close and lets us go; God gives us self-awareness and freedom, that most eloquent of God-given gifts, which occasions a vulnerability in God himself.

In a time and place in which women had almost no power, when Israel lived under the oppressive scrutiny of Roman rule, Mary opened herself to God's Holy Spirit and became a pivotal collaborator in the work of salvation. She stood against the secular and religious authorities of her day: the secular King Herod who would make every effort to kill Jesus in infancy, and the religious leaders who would plot with Pilate to orchestrate his ruin decades later.

The fact that God chose pregnancy and birth as the medium of salvation—not a dramatic apparition in the sky, not a cataclysmic event in nature, but the mundane normalcy of a pregnant woman, something we see everyday without comment—tells us a great deal about how God deals with humanity. God draws us to himself through our own human desiring and the concrete reality of our lives. God's love is certainly greater than created reality, but it is also immanent, coming from within created reality. A spirituality of pregnancy and childbirth is a way to get in touch with the ongoing nature of God's creative work and the collaborative nature of that work. Can we believe that we too are invited to collaborate with God?

ENCOUNTER AND PRACTICE

Encounter

In pregnancy, we collaborate in God's work of ongoing creation by allowing the Lord to knit another human being within our womb. When we separate from our baby in giving birth, it is the start of letting go as our child grows up. From birth on, we place our child back into God's arms, knowing that the end goal is his or her independence. In this meditation, we rest with the psalms in order to reflect that we, like our children, are God's handiwork, and continue to belong to God.

1. Set aside twenty minutes. Read some poetry or listen to some music in order to relax your mind. Transition out of the concerns of your day and into the present moment. Ready your body by breathing deeply ten to fifteen times, and feeling the sensation as air enters and leaves your lungs. When you are ready, go to the next step.
2. Read Psalm 34, 62, or 63, or Luke 1:47–55. Here is part of Psalm 34:

I will bless the LORD at all times;
   his praise shall continually be in my mouth.
My soul makes its boast in the LORD;
   let the humble hear and be glad.
O magnify the LORD with me,
   and let us exalt his name together.

I sought the LORD and he answered me,
   and delivered me from all my fears.
Look to him and be radiant;
   so your faces will never be ashamed....

O taste and see that the LORD is good;
    happy are those who take refuge in him." (Ps 34:1–5, 8)

3. Which line of the psalm touches you most? Rest with it and let other thoughts come and go.
4. How does the passage make you feel? What new thoughts came up for you? What are your desires at this moment: desires for yourself, your child or children, your husband, your friends, anyone you may be thinking of today? Share your feelings, thoughts, and desires with God.
5. End with a prayer of thanksgiving.

Practice

1. *Listening to the Wind*. Every afternoon my dog, Jessie, needs a walk. My children, too young to stay home alone, come along. One day, when the constant chatter and running in circles got to be enough, I asked my children to sit down with me and listen to the wind. After a minute or two of greatly needed quiet, they told me the things they heard in the wind.

    It can be a relief to listen and be still for a moment. The sound of wind and water soothe us and help us rest. For this exercise, which can be done by yourself or with children, take one minute or so to listen to the wind (or look at a flower, gaze into the night sky, examine the different shades of green in plants, listen to the rain, feel the breeze, and so on). Focus your senses on one thing. Afterward, think about what you felt, heard, saw, smelled, or tasted. Give thanks to God for the experience of creation of which you are a part.

2. *Finding Inner Strength*. Sit down with a piece of paper and a pencil, along with colored pencils or paints and a brush. Sketch or paint an image in answer to one of the questions below. Choose

whichever question strikes you at this moment: What will labor look like for me? What does my fear, hesitation, or doubt look like? Who do I want to be present with me when I am most vulnerable (in labor or at other times)? What do I look like when I am being supported? What does the picture of my last labor look like? How do I feel when I am in companionship with Mary or other women? What does God look like "giving birth to the world"? When you are finished, spend some time looking at your image. What does it reveal about you? If you wish, offer this part of yourself to God.

CHAPTER THREE

Love as You Are Loved

Mother as Nurturer

Can a woman forget her nursing child,
   or show no compassion for the child of her womb?
Even these may forget,
   yet I will not forget you.
See, I have inscribed you on the palms of my hands.
Isaiah 49:15

In her inspiring book on family life, Wendy Wright reminds us of where the sacred is found on a daily basis. She writes, "Blessedly, family life is not just about doing....It is first and foremost about the intense and tender and often fierce interrelatedness of human beings. It is about the astonishment of being with each other."[1] Each of us experiences this "being together" in our families and in countless other human relationships that fill our lives. When our children are infants, we have the chance to drink deeply of being together. We spend our time gazing at our baby, loving his or her uniqueness and reveling in presence, intimacy, and love. It is indeed amazing, and we are spellbound by the wonder of our child's uniqueness and beauty. Despite the overwhelming challenges and the sleepless nights, our child's preciousness is what impacts us most in the first year of parenting: the astonishment of being together!

Our personal uniqueness and our interrelatedness are central to what it means to be human. Life binds us to the mundane, however, and we routinely ignore the beauty of this astounding truth. Impatience, weariness, physical limitations, and work distract us and blind us to our own and others' sacredness. Instead of celebrating being together, we may find ourselves, especially as mothers, yearning to get away and being overwhelmed by the claims made on us. How can we discover wonder and find the sacred and restful contemplation in being together, when being together is often the very source of our exhaustion?[2] How can we pay better attention to those times when we do manage to see through the mundane and glimpse what is underneath: God, self-revealing, in the person we love and in our own love returned?

In this chapter, we will look at motherhood as a vocation of love, specifically nurturing love. Three questions will be considered:

1. How do women today experience the nurturing role?
2. How does God model the Mother-Nurturer?
3. How do our children nurture us back to God?

WHAT DOES NURTURING MEAN TODAY?

Nurture can be a scary word for a mother. It may conjure up visions of a goddess figure in a flowing gown, effortlessly pouring forth love with abandon and joy, heedless of herself, wanting only to feed, clothe, and tend her many children. When we contrast this with the daily marathon of our lives and the worries and work we know to be our reality, we can only roll our eyes. Women have a healthy mistrust of this and more subtle images of romanticized motherhood. We distrust them because idealizing motherhood has led too many women down the road of disappointment and despair. Despite our mistrust, we may fall into more contemporary traps of false mother-images. Popular culture has continued to romanticize motherhood, offering new objects for us to admire and swoon over. The media gives us the ideal of the Amazon mother who can "do it all" and "have it all." It presents celebrity moms as the new diva-goddess, always sexy, always available, and, oh yes, always profitably employed. In contrast, the media also gives us the tragedy of the mothers who fail in big ways and small, those who wind up on the evening news because their child suffered abuse at a daycare center. We are assailed by an endless supply of "mother dramas" and of advice about what to do and not do raising our children. Together, these images created by the media contain the not-so-subtle insinuation that we should be perfect.[3]

Little of this cultural hoopla helps real women. The vast majority of mothers are primarily concerned with practical issues. As a matter of necessity, we tend to be concrete in our thinking rather than abstract. In each generation we struggle and find ways to articulate what we need to mother successfully in a given context. Today is no different. Women's presence in the professional world, in politics, and in public life strengthens our capacity to clarify our position. Contrary to what might appear "unfeminine," our assertiveness has actually served to further our ability to care for those entrusted to us in a concrete way, the only way that matters. We care about human issues because they directly affect our ability to nurture our children, providing for their health, nutrition, housing, and education—as well as a clean environment, security and peace, freedom from coercion and interference, and, even more basically, the right to life itself.[4] All of these issues are not simply "political," but are bound together in a mother's heart as elements of her children's well-being. They are unavoidable facts of daily life. Motherhood is the nurturing hub of life.

Let us define the term *nurturing*. *Nurture* has broader meaning than simply "to feed," for it includes all that fosters growth: "to promote the development by providing nourishment, support, encouragement, etc., during the stages of growth." It also means "to bring up; train; educate."[5] To nurture another person is to foster physical, spiritual, and emotional-psychological *development*. To be more specific still, it includes all the human issues named above plus the more interpersonal ones that are required to meet the needs of a human person. This definition places the emphasis on the concrete requirements of nurturing. Education, for example, is not simply a value or a policy, but a boy or a girl in a classroom, whose mind is developing and who is receiving care and attention from those who collaborate to facilitate learning. In a similar way, parenting is not a system or a program, but a series of human interactions that actually form, mold, educate, and train a child. Discipline can only take place through the intentional, focused attention that a mother and father give to the development of virtue in their children. It is ongoing. (It is important to note that while the child is taught through the discipline that a parent delivers, the parent also learns about his or her own sense of self, about values, self-control, and the capacity to love. We will return later to the mutuality inherent in nurturing.) The sustained attention that nurturing requires at each stage of development is the core of parental love. Thus, to nurture is to love another person with the intention of enabling that person to reach wholeness.

It is a struggle to love in this way. Mothers and others who are dedicated to hands-on care of children put great effort into nurturing them, for it requires selfless giving. Ours is not a world that esteems selfless giving. In fact, the ethos of our time and place seems to be "take, not give." Deep dissatisfaction results from living in a "take culture." Material things have no power to nurture, and yet we easily act as if they do. This can leave us with the uneasy feeling that we are surrounded by stuff instead of by loving, nurturing people. The actual value of a material gift depends entirely on the intention of the giver who may offer a thing as a token of love, in indifference, or even as a substitute for love. The allure of a Crate and Barrel living room or a Pottery Barn bedroom, the constant siren song of the next new toy, can be obstacles, making us less aware of our true intentions and of the need to foster family relationships.

Paying attention to what is in our heart as we give can transform the material world into an offering of love. Mystics have sung of the beauty of creation as the very gift of God, by which God communicates his love to us. In this context, we can freely rejoice in the giving and receiving of material things. All that is beautiful and good is at our disposal to use as offerings of nurturing love to others. The art that children create is a great reminder to us of the simple offering that is part of the landscape of family life. That art goes on the wall or is hung on the refrigerator. Words and pictures tell the story of belonging, of having security and comfort. At other times, the words and pictures may relate sorrow, fear, or conflict. All of this is accepted in the nurturing environment where gifts are exchanged in the spirit of mutual trust. Imagine the setting that welcomes a newborn child: the crib and blankets carefully knitted, the small plush toy. Outside the window a garden has been tended and its greens and yellows play in the light coming through the window. The sun shines on the child. The mother, the father, the welcoming friends and relatives shine in another way—with a resolved intention to care for this child into the future. The beauty of the picture we are imagining finds its true importance as a symbolic expression of nurturing love. The so-called nesting instinct is a manifestation of this, for it drives a person to create instinctually a space of beauty, which welcomes and fosters spiritual-psychological well-being, our own and our child's. The home we create and the gifts we exchange make visible the care in our hearts.

While the home serves as a sanctuary for a young child's development, home is a temporary respite. Nurturing love eventually follows a child out into the world. It is not enough to see nurturing love as a "private" affair. A mother tends to know "the history and cost of human flesh."[6] Women have tended to remember the cost because they survive when their husbands and sons die in war. They have the memory of it etched in their beings, handed down like a memorial. The image of the *Pietà*, of Mary holding her son, Jesus, in the moments after he is taken down from the cross, reminds us what is at stake. Whether we are talking about the life of our child, the life of the children of others, or the life of the earth itself—life is our business and we know its fragility. This is part of the reality of our mothering love, and while we are mercifully often unconscious of it, nurturing love has this edge to it. We nurture out of urgency to preserve and foster life in a world where life is threatened at every turn. As the saying goes, it is dangerous to be alive. To nurture then is not only an expression of sustained love, but of loving in the awareness of risk, loss, and danger. Mothers do not live in a bubble; our homes are not absolute sanctuaries but temporary ones. We must live exposed, and we are very aware too of our children's exposure and the need to equip them to live in this world.

Nurturing therefore requires courage. Courage enables us to love in the first place and prepares us especially to love as mothers. It is not unusual to harbor a simplistic understanding of love, as if it were natural or easy. Love is work. Love is art. It is learning the act of commitment to another's well-being for the long term, even to the point of becoming vulnerable oneself for their sake. So this next insight extends our definition of nurturing further: it is, as we have said, a form of love that is given faithfully during all the stages of a child's development, but it is also done with the intention of letting go at the culmination of that formation. It is formative love that sets free the object of our love.

When a son or daughter moves out of the home, when parents send a son or daughter off to college or to a job in another city, it is a profoundly moving experience. Over the years a mother and a father have let their child scoot further and further away, into the hardness of the world, and the very success of their parenting leads to this jumping-off point. It is at once exhilarating and terrifying. One mother described her leave-taking as a mixture of "pride, sorrow, joy, grief, anxiety, and relief." That same mother had this memory to share: as she walked at sunset at her daughter's campus, engulfed in these conflicting emotions, she came upon a statue of a woman. It was a statue of Mary unlike any she had seen before. Mary stood tall, holding her infant son high in her arms toward the sky in a gesture that expressed the "protective love of motherhood that must relinquish to an unknown future that which is more precious to her than life itself." The dedication inscribed at the base of the statue was "to the mothers of the university's students."[7] This image of Mary as a mother, loving and offering in the same gesture, is a powerful reminder of the heroism inherent in mothering love. Mary's gesture represents each little effort of patience, empathy, discipline, and care as an investment in our children's personhood, in a future which is wholly theirs, yet which we participate in by our nurturing love, forming them today for the tasks of tomorrow.

GOD MODELS THE MOTHER-NURTURER

Isaiah uses many contradictory metaphors to describe our relationship to God. Images of tenderness and love are prevalent, especially in the second and third sections of the book, describing the exile of Israel in Babylon. God reminds the people that he is "the rock from which you were hewn...the quarry from which you were dug" (Isaiah 51:1). The metaphor of rock has a raw quality to it, as if the people were sculpted out of the very being of God. How many artists carve their work out of the material of their very existence? This is a vivid portrayal of our origin in God! The quarry image also carries the connotation of ongoing formation, through God's graciously given providence. It is echoed in references to Israel being formed "in the womb" (Isa 44:2, 24; Ps 139). In these chapters Isaiah gives us a portrait of God as Mother-Nurturer. This is the aspect of God's love that manifests itself through sustained providence, a love that engulfs our lives and forms us according to our needs at different times. In this it reflects the nurturing love of a mother. Three aspects of the love identified in Isaiah are its unconditional nature that relentlessly accepts the people back even when they turn away from the Lord; its mercy that offers comfort and deliverance when the people are being tested; and, finally, the celebration and delight that come from sharing the life of God in God's family, a free and generous gift.

In Isaiah, the Lord reminds Israel that as his people they belong to God alone. The imagery of carrying Israel in the womb, birthing her, and loving her tenderly presents for us the image of God as Mother and the impossibility of Israel belonging to anyone else. There is no mistaking the maternity of a child. The whole question of idolatry has to do with this question of belonging. In a tirade against false gods, the Lord challenges Israel's apparent ignorance of their God: "Woe to anyone who says to a father, 'What are you begetting?' or to a woman, 'With what are you in labor?'" (Isa 45:10). Elsewhere God likens himself to a woman in the agony of labor for Israel (Isa 42:14), as one who cries out and can no longer hold back. The book ends with a lengthy metaphor of mother Zion in whom God begets and mothers his people (Isa 66:6–14). All of this culminates in one consoling message: you are mine. As we read in chapter 43,

> But now thus says the LORD,
>   he who created you, O Jacob,
>   he who formed you, O Israel:
> Do not fear, for I have redeemed you;
>   I have called you by name and you are mine....
> You are precious in my sight,
>   and honored, and I love you. (Isa 43:1, 4a)

No matter how far Israel strays, nothing will change the fact of her being the Lord's daughter.

The rich imagery in these passages impresses upon the mind and heart every person's need for unconditional love. Idolatry represents false love while the Lord offers lasting love. We experience that love directly but also through each other, in our family and community. As parents, we participate in this by building a foundation at the beginning of life. A mother or father's constant care for a baby speaks to that child, saying: *You belong; you are a part of this family, and here you are safe and accepted. When you face adversity, we will not abandon you.* This first step in nurturing our children, providing a sense of love without conditions, would seem to be the most difficult, and yet parents offer it almost without thinking. When in some circumstances this early love is missing, the consequences can be dire. In contrast, when "you are mine" becomes a deeply rooted conviction in a child's life, it provides spiritual and psychological security, which is the foundation for continued growth. This basic psychological need is usually met early in life through hours holding our children, feeding them, meeting all their needs, responding to them with consistent care.

The intimacy a child experiences within the family will later be linked to his or her readiness to negotiate the world outside the family. As the child grows and begins to negotiate an unfamiliar and sometimes dangerous world, that inner security will form a nucleus of inner strength, a force to help the child negotiate life's difficulty and pain. Thus, while unconditional love would seem to be an ideal rather than the norm, it is something a new mother does instinctively, if imperfectly. A mother's or father's early caretaking is the essential foundation for the ongoing development upon which all further nurturing love will be built. This love, so beautifully expressed in Isaiah, is a holy love in which every parent participates, when they care for their child in this generous way.

The second aspect of nurturing love in Isaiah involves testing and deliverance. God describes his relationship to Israel as that of a parent, dedicated to the point of folly to the well-being of a sometimes ungrateful and disobedient child:

> When you pass through the waters, I will be with you;
>   and through the rivers, they shall not overwhelm you;
> when you walk through the fire, you shall not be burned,
>   and the flame shall not consume you. (Isa 43:2)

In other passages God shows restraint when Israel is tested: "I am the LORD your God who teaches you for your own good, who leads you in the way you should go" (Isa 48:17). The parental image of God is one of patience, as God takes back his wayward child over and over, remembering his love and urging his people to be faithful. What Israel learns through this process is central to its maturity and growth. The sorrow of exile in Babylon and the difficulties God's people must endure are part of a desert experience, but it is only through that experience that they learn to walk and grow to maturity.

None of us needs to invent tests for our children. Life is full of them. As parents, our hope is that we can help them through what life throws at them with as little personal cost as possible. If we want them to learn, however, we must allow them to experiment, to fail, and to finally succeed on their own. If we do everything for them, protect them from every fall or mistake, they will not learn. Instead of growing, they will be at a disadvantage because they will not have learned self-reliance. When our children suffer, when they feel alone or must face some difficulty or discipline, it is often tempting to rush in to their rescue. Yet if we allow them to make the decisions appropriate to their age, and let them experiment with what happens when they don't do what is asked of them, they will learn to stand on their own two feet. We imitate God's love by our presence and encouragement and guidance.

Empathy is an important aspect of loving a child during difficult moments.[8] Preschool and early elementary-age children suffer under what seem to us small, inconsequential events, like the sudden cancellation of a play date or a rained out birthday party. They explode with emotion for what we would call "nothing." Because they do not yet have the tools to manage their feelings, they cannot hold back their disappointment and grief. They feel deeply and suddenly, and their own emotions can be scary to them. At this age, children also want to assert themselves as separate from their parents, hence their fascination with the word "no." If we understand what is going on in them, it is easier to see what a misbehaving child needs, to experience the consequences of his or her behavior along with the reassurance that he or she is loved despite the failure. This empathy can be quite difficult for parents. It requires that we first understand the experience our child is having, next that we put aside our impatience and judgment, and finally that we take the time to "suffer with" (the literal meaning of *empathize*) our child who must accept the consequences.

As our children grow up, they depend on us less and less; we may begin to feel more like managers than nurturers. Despite their apparent aloofness, our children will continue to need acceptance and empathy in countless situations that life throws at them. They need us to continue to nurture them into adulthood in new ways. Self-acceptance is a lifelong challenge, and

the freedom that comes with humble self-esteem is a key factor
in a child's future well-being and success. Parents stop nurturing
their children with the milk of constant attention that they need
while they are small, but the honey of our reassurance of their
goodness is something they will need into maturity: "You are
precious and I love you" (Isa 43:4). This comfort is reflected in
Isaiah's portrayal of God who gives water and nourishment.

God's deliverance often reaches a climax in a feast and in
thanksgiving:

> Ho, everyone who thirsts,
>   come to the waters;
> and you that have no money,
>   come, buy and eat!
> Come buy wine and milk
>   without money and without price.
> Why do you spend your money for that which is not
>   bread,
>   and your labor for that which does not satisfy?
>   (Isa 55:1–2a)

And this:

> The LORD will guide you continually,
>   and satisfy your needs in parched places,
>   and make your bones strong;
> and you shall be like a watered garden,
>   like a spring of water
>   whose waters never fail. (Isa 58:11)

The third aspect of nurturing love in Isaiah is of celebration
and delight at sharing a life together as God's free and generous
gift. During the ordeals his people must face, God offers consolation by meeting practical needs: "They did not thirst when he
led them through the deserts; he made water flow for them from
the rock." (Isa 48:21) In the midst of hardship, the people need
nourishment to keep going and comfort to not lose heart. And
when the ordeal has ended, God "will make her wilderness like
Eden, her desert like the garden of the LORD; joy and gladness

will be found in her, thanksgiving and the voice of song" (Isa 51:3–4).

Notice that God provides food and drink to people who are unable to meet their own needs. Jesus proclaimed his gospel in this same spirit, quoting Isaiah 61:1–2: "The spirit of the Lord GOD is upon me…he has sent me to bring good news to the oppressed, to bind up the brokenhearted…to comfort all who mourn" (cf. In Luke 4:18). "God feeding the destitute" is a prevalent theme in Scripture. God gave Israel manna in the desert and provided water from the rock to slake her thirst. The tradition of sharing the Eucharist proclaims our need for God and our ultimate hunger for God over all else. Manna was called "food from heaven," and as our benefactor, God allows us to share in his life, receiving all we have as gift.

So much of mothering work involves food and drink. From the first day we nurse our baby to the gallons of milk we buy our teenage sons, and through all the nutritious meals and snacks in between, we are constantly offering "good food." In her book chronicling her years of motherhood, Denise Roy says: "For two decades I have broken bread, poured grape juice, preached, prayed, told stories, bestowed blessings, taken care of the sick, heard confessions. I have been a parent. These have been the sacraments of my daily life."[9] Roy's overtly priestly depiction of her mothering shows that the kind of "feeding" which we do nourishes our children on many levels—that physical nourishment is only a part of how we nourish. We minister to the whole person of our child. Nursing is a good example of this, for it nourishes body and spirit, the body with nutrients and the spirit with security and peace. When we feed our children in the literal sense, we constantly make evident the deeper need and thirst we all share.

God promises to satisfy our hunger and thirst, offering comfort in our needs (Isa 51:3–4). Thanksgiving has been for me an image of the kingdom of heaven. One particular Thanksgiving Day gathering at the home of a dear friend was especially memorable. There were some fifty people around one table, from all walks of life, different ethnicities and social classes—all sharing company and food, all giving thanks. The variety and delectability of the food we shared had an intangible counterpart that also "fed" us, the communion among diverse people gathered to give thanks. After the meal we each took a turn to express what we were most grateful for during the preceding year. The year itself—the concrete, historical details of so many lives—became the banquet of our gratitude, another spiritual gift. This was a precious moment of kingdom love for me, a reality already present in germ, around a table of people gathered to simply share food and gratitude.

Isaiah leaves us with a fresh sense of the importance and beauty of the nurturing role. Remembering our own need to be nurtured is a powerful starting point, as we attempt to parent with the same love. As God continues to nurture us through life, we can find consolation in the fact that we belong to God who is with us during our own trials, who nourishes us and invites us to share God's own table where joy is shared as food.

SEEING THROUGH THE EYES OF A CHILD

Living with children has many joys and challenges. They charm us and exert a powerful claim on us that we cannot deny. They make us laugh and surprise us; they sometimes bore us with endless questions and talk about their concerns. Spending extended amounts of time with children can be maddening. Theirs is a perspective and a way of seeing the world that is not always easy for us to connect with. As adults, we resist paying attention to the world as they see it, because we have grown accustomed to adult ways of acting, thinking, and viewing everything. This is our way of negotiating the world we live in and providing for our families. However, children can teach us about ourselves and remind us of treasures we may have left behind on our way to adulthood, like playfulness, wonder, raw emotion, and nobility. Further, when we pay attention to them, children can help us come closer to realizing our true relationship to God.

Jesus had a surprising response to children. The gospel tells us that he blessed the infants and children brought to him. His disciples, however, stepped in to rebuke those carrying the children to Jesus. The word *rebuke* does not indicate a polite, little "Move along, now." It comes from an old French word meaning "to beat back." When Jesus saw what they were doing, he was indignant. He abruptly stopped, called his disciples, and made them gather around him. Picture them sitting at his feet like children at circle time, a reversal of the importance Jesus' disciples routinely placed on themselves! Then, the Lord beckoned a child over to stand in front of everyone, a position given only to a teacher. Jesus looked hard at his disciples and told them, "Do not stop [these children from coming to me]; for it is to such as these that the kingdom of God belongs. Truly, I tell you, whoever does not receive the kingdom of God as a little child will never enter it." And Jesus embraced the children, "took them up in his arms, laid his hands on them, and blessed them" (Mark 10:14–16).

There is nothing sentimental about this passage. It is a challenge, and what is at stake is nothing less than the kingdom of God. Access to that kingdom requires that we trust and allow ourselves to be blessed and embraced by Jesus. Possessing it is a matter of the heart, and only through the heart can we can gain access to it. St. Paul calls it "righteousness and peace and joy in the Holy Spirit" (Romans 14:17). Elsewhere Jesus likens the kingdom to a pearl of great price, the celebration of a son reconciled with his family, the feasting at a wedding, an investment given in trust so it might grow. These images describe it as a priceless treasure freely given out of love and out of mercy, with a rejoicing spirit and in esteeming trust toward a loyal servant.

What are we meant to understand from Jesus' words about the kingdom belonging to children? His ultimatum ("whoever does not...will never") contains a clue about his whole life and mission. Jesus is angered when the disciples assume the children are unworthy and their presence is an interference, because the disciples are showing yet again that they have not yet understood the nature of their own relationship to God. How many times had he told his followers, the last would be first? How often had he repeated they were not to seek to lord it over each other self-importantly? (Matt 20:24). Jesus did something ridiculous when he made the men sit down and stood the child in their midst as teacher! In a culture where women, children, and slaves were considered possessions, it must have been altogether too much for them. The position of the child standing in their midst was an unmistakable sign that God's kingdom will not be earned or apprehended by Jesus' followers through their own will and intellect. If children possess God's kingdom, then it must not depend on any special ability, mental acumen, or particular trait.

This points to some important differences between adults and children. Adults are customarily in a "knowing mode" while children are in the "learning mode." The way adults interact with other adults, compared to the way we interact with children, demonstrates this. When we meet other adults, we find out what they are proficient at, what their careers and hobbies are, what they know about current events, and generally what they think. When we meet children, we do things with them—Frisbee, arts and crafts, that kind of thing. Conversation is based on the world of the child's experience, not expertise. Adults also tend to analyze, while children trust their instincts. For example, when adults go shopping for a new product, we analyze information to get the most for our money and to determine that the item is right for us. In contrast, children must operate out of trust. Since they cannot know enough to make complex choices for themselves, they must habitually accept and believe the goodness of options they are given by others.

Interaction with children gives us the opportunity to operate on a different level, in the realm of experience and trust. At rare times when we can detach from our concerns and can enjoy being together, we can find freedom in leaving behind the adult knowing and analyzing mode and enter the world of being teachable and trusting.

This ability is necessary for our spiritual growth. Too often the knowing and analyzing mode dampens our sense of wonder. Children can revive this in us. Because they are learners, they can more readily receive God and the gift of the kingdom. They have not yet put up barriers against wonder and trust. It is interesting to note that children resist their own status as learners. Many mothers report that toddlers in their car seats insist they know how to buckle up saying, "I do! I do!" And children love to portray themselves as already knowing everything there is to know! Yet, behind this facade, wonder is the habitual home of children, and the world still fascinates them. They are enthralled with nature, with a million new things. It is wonderful when we can put down our guard and share their amazement.

Seeing "through a child's eyes" in the gospel sense means we allow them to mirror back to us our true relationship to God, and then to trust it and wonder at it. This is what we are: children of God! "We are beloved not because of what we do. We are beloved because of who we are."[10] God loves us by sharing with us everything, his own divine life and the entire cosmos of the created world: the All of nature, the All of the universe, the All of the macro- and microcosmic infinity of What Is—held out as a priceless inheritance that God asks us to keep as faithful stewards and to gather back to God when the time comes. This All is truly a wonder! Yet, how seldom do we remember who we are and what God gives us. Children nurture us back to God by helping us experience ourselves as learners and find wonder as we behold the All of creation. They nurture us by their own constant trust, which is directed to us so completely, despite our failures and inadequacy as parents.

People who work among the poor, among refugees, and among others in need often report an astonishing experience. They feel consolation and are deeply touched by those to whom they minister. In the same way, our children can nurture us back to God. In the simplicity of giving to another, we receive from this interaction a mysterious grace. God breaks into the mundane and gives us resurgence of our inner life.

Motherhood is not a job. It is a way of life. We seem to choose motherhood, but in reality it chooses us. Flinders describes a kind of law that surfaces from the collective experience of the women saints she writes about: "You don't have to go out looking for your calling, because it will be quite apparent to you once you have, in the words of Gandhi, 'gotten yourself out of the way.'" A calling cannot be left behind at the end of a busy day. We can't prop up our feet and rest from being who-we-are. Nor docs a calling depend on remuneration. On the contrary, "payment" sometimes takes the form of social invisibility. Our work is marked by the lesson in piety Jesus repeated after each lesson on Christian practice and prayer: "Your Father who sees in secret will repay you." Nurturing is our present, everyday task, Flinders continues, "placed where you all but trip over it, [which] will make it indisputably yours and no one else's."[11] It is our great gift to know that we are loved and nurtured even as we nurture our children.

ENCOUNTER AND PRACTICE

Encounter

> A mother's service is nearest, readiest, and surest. It is nearest because it is most natural. It is readiest because it is most loving. And it is surest because it is most true. This office no one but God alone might or could ever have performed to the full....It is [God] who does the mothering through the creatures by whom it is done. *Julian of Norwich*[12]

After reading the above passage, take one of the attributes of God's love described in the Book of Isaiah, which were mentioned earlier in this chapter:

- God looks upon us as precious and honored.
- We come from God's own being and are destined to return to God.
- God delivers us from every ordeal, comforts us, and promises to be with us.
- God feeds us with the food of heaven and satisfies us.

At the beginning of your prayer time, ask for the grace to experience God's mothering love. As you pray, imagine how you came from God like a rock from a quarry or a child from the womb and how you belong to God as a beloved child.

Practice

1. *Nurture Yourself.* In order to love our neighbor, we need to practice a patient love for ourselves. The way we treat ourselves spills over into our treatment of others. Sometimes as mothers we give too much of ourselves. This may cause feelings of resentment. In this practice, the assignment is to notice where in your work or daily family life you may routinely be doing something for others that you resent. Offer your feelings to God and ask for the grace to give away your resentment. Give thanks to God and ask for help to change your behavior and take better care of yourself according to God's will. Be ready to either shift that work to a helper or do the task in a different spirit. Notice if and how your feelings or attitude change as a result of this short exercise.

2. *Give Thanks: Saying Grace After Dinner.* It is a tradition in the Church to pray before and after meals. Before dinner, say a very short grace. Save this prayer below for the end of dinner, perhaps before desert (this will keep attention at the table). It is too hard for little ones to compose thoughts when they are running on empty. Read one of the readings below and ask your children the questions following it.

Reading 1: Psalm 145:15–16. "The eyes of all look to you and you give them their food in due season. You open your hand, satisfying the desire of every living thing."

Questions:
- Does all our food come from God?
- How does God feed other living things?
- What does it mean to "look to God" to satisfy our desires?

Reading 2:
We cannot love God unless we love each other,
And to love each other we must know each other
In the breaking of bread, and we are not alone anymore.
Heaven is a banquet and life is a banquet too,
Even with a crust, where there is companionship.
Love comes with community. *Dorothy Day*[13]

Questions:
- How do we get to know each other "in the breaking of bread"?
- What does "life is a banquet" mean?
- Do you think you could enjoy a crust of bread if you were eating with people you love or your very best friend?
- Do you ever forget to eat? What makes you forget?

CHAPTER FOUR

Do Not Be Afraid
How Love Casts Out Fear

> How very good and pleasant it is
> when kindred live together in unity!
> It is like the precious oil on the head....
> It is like the dew of Hermon,
> which falls on the mountains of Zion.
> For there the LORD ordained his blessing,
> life forevermore.
>
> Psalm 133

Fear is one of the principle obstacles each of us faces as we attempt to faithfully live out our calling. A calling is a process, and no matter how intensely we say yes to God at the beginning of our journey, through life's daily obstacles, struggles, and doubts, God draws us to an even deeper commitment. This process takes courage. We are hindered by fears, both conscious and unconscious, that can block our path forward. These fears cannot easily be dispelled or willed away. They are part of the normal landscape of our lives, part of our human lot. What can we do with our fear?

God invites us to trust specifically in relation to our particular vocation. It is another way of saying, "Go forward in your calling despite the obstacles you face. Confront the resistance within you, your doubt and hesitance." Fear is like a plank in our eye, blocking our view of what God wills for us, and flattening the godly desires God is nurturing in our hearts. It may make us feel the urge to run away, like Jonah, who ran from God at the very moment when his true calling became most apparent. Our fears cause us to waste time, doubt ourselves, and isolate. They breed false humility, which is often a nice safe place to be. The idea that God might have work for *you* to accomplish may be too challenging. However, going forward despite fear enables us to take risks, become more aware of our calling, and engage with God in a responsive collaboration to build the kingdom of heaven.

Fear is treacherous territory for mothers. In an earlier chapter, the fear of failure was considered, how the transition to motherhood changes our whole world, jeopardizing our sense of control, limiting our independence, and disturbing our notion of success. We step into a new role that can be frightening. In order for us to take on the responsibility and authority of motherhood, it is important to see it as a calling that God equips us to live out to its fullest potential. Often this involves not trying harder or "getting it right," but trusting in God and in ourselves as called by God. This trust is at the heart of overcoming fear. Examining our basic attitude toward motherhood and family life will help us uncover our fears (whether conscious and unconscious), and cast them out.

How is motherhood perceived? For many, motherhood includes the relationship of a committed marriage. For believers, participating in the sacrament of marriage is a declaration that the relationship into which we hope to bring children is one that is also a sign of eternal, divine love. We witness in marriage to the faithful love of God for the entirety of humanity. Into this love of two, we receive a child as a gift. Though the technical advances of modern fertility treatments may cause us to forget, the truth is that a child is always a gift from the creative love of God. This reality places us as mothers in a relationship of stewardship to our children, whose destiny is glory. Through and in the life they lead in our care, we are forming them to perceive that they are not only our children, but also children of the light, children of God.

These beliefs may seem exalted or too abstract to help us in daily life. However, they can affect our attitudes and how we actually see ourselves and our families. They can impact the way we organize our lives and educate our children. Motherhood as a Christian vocation is transcendent, for it takes us out of ourselves and places us at the service of the kingdom of heaven for the sake of our children. Many women experience the need to explore faith and spirituality at the time they are having babies or when their children are young. The gift of a child makes us want to open up to the transcendence of our own new reality as mothers.

Rather than being motivated by our own needs alone or distracted by indulging our hidden fears, faith summons us to put our focus elsewhere: not on the mistakes we might make, but on the privileges we are afforded; not on the unknown future, but on the gift of the present; not on the contingency of this life, but on the connection between the here and now and the lasting kingdom God promises. Understanding the dynamics of fear and how we react can help us see how to respond with greater faith—can free us to live more completely this calling.

WE EACH HAVE A FEAR-HISTORY

Fear is expressed and felt differently depending on personality types, but the roots of fear are universal. We naturally fear suffering and death, and their harbingers: emotional and physical pain, illness, anxiety, uncertainty, contingency, the unknown, even phantoms we invent all on our own. On a more mundane level, we fear anything that undermines continued security. So, in daily life we want to know where our family's next meal is coming from, that our housing is secure, that our job will still be there when we return from vacation, and that our kids have opportunities in their future. There are other, more psychological aspects of security that affect us as well. These have to do with status and the ego, how we feel about ourselves, about our relationships with others, whether we feel accepted, loved, or worthy.

Human vulnerability is something we experience from childhood. I remember as a small girl, I watched my father, a restaurant owner, as he was cutting meat. He sliced his finger badly and bled quite a bit. I suddenly felt: how fragile life is! How thin the thread between health and injury, life and death! At that moment, realizing that I myself and every other human being shared my father's vulnerability, I wanted to grasp onto something that was not contingent. Another memory from childhood came from my mother, who often told us that if we could see God, we would not be able to do anything else but love God. We would choose God above all else and desire to be with God. This made sense to me. It soothed in some small way the vertigo of life's contingency. God's beauty and goodness were there, even if the darkness of faith didn't allow me to see it clearly. Knowing there was something Real, Someone greater than me and the world, offered the psychological ground on which I could build my personal, lasting security. God was goodness and life, and this could enable me to go forward into risk-taking with the courage that life would summon from within me.

Our childhood sets the stage for how we will deal with our fear and insecurity throughout life. Normally our parents give us our initial sense of safety, belonging, and love. Eventually, however, we must look past our parents to find our own touchstone of security. When the Word of Scripture enjoins us, "Do not be afraid," it means that God knows our most intimate fears and worries, that he wishes to console us and to welcome us into the realm of trust. Putting our trust in God is not simply a psychological security blanket. In fact, tragedy and hardship can make us doubt the very goodness of God that originally gave us comfort. But the orientation of our lives toward God remains. It is solely because God has revealed his love to us that we can cast off fear in its totality. Faith in God's power, expressed in love and fidelity, is at the root of the courage that enables us to do this.

LOVE COUNTERACTS FEAR

Love works against fear. "There is no fear in love, but perfect love casts out fear. We love because he first loved us" (1 John 4:18a, 19). The fact that God loved us first is the starting point of Christian spirituality. John, after telling us not to fear judgment, links our victory over fear to a very specific action: loving others, "for those who do not love a brother or sister whom they have seen, cannot love God whom they have not seen."

At its root, family life is a school of love. However, attitudes, such as competitiveness, can seep into family life, play into our fears, and make them grow. Teresa of Avila used to call these attitudes "hateful comparisons." Consumer society tends to drive us to be more, do more, own more than others. We can get caught up in feelings of never being, doing, or having enough. Another fearful attitude is individualism. One aspect of this is to assume the family is a secretive and private realm, with neither responsibility toward others nor claims made on the broader society. The message is, "you are on your own." This might cause us to forget those in need when we are successful, and to fail to ask for help when we ourselves suffer or are in need of compassion and support. The two responses are related, two sides of the same coin, for if we assume it is a sign of weakness to ask for help, we are not likely to help others who need it. Individualism causes us to refuse any meaningful responsibility for others.

Fear is a springboard for sin in both these cases. Perfect love in God shows us just the opposite. The more we wholeheartedly love, the more rooted we are in the one who "loved us first," and thus the Holy Spirit can set us free from fearful attitudes. For the pitfalls of competitive striving, individualism, and other stumbling blocks are remedied gradually, in the practice of love through the countless commitments inherent in family and social life. These commitments throw us headlong into the tasks of love. The tasks of love are the soil into which the Word of God falls, a fertile and rich soil that allows our spiritual lives to bloom. It also heightens our awareness of the vulnerability and contingency we share. As a school of love, family prepares us to love beyond ourselves and to become more oriented toward compassion and toward care of the poor and of the earth. It is a dynamic that urges us outward, not in on ourselves.

A mother's focus on caring for children drives us toward relationship building. This can be a lifelong exercise in relinquishing fear and welcoming perfect love. The concrete situations of daily life summon us to learn to emulate God's mothering love. We open up to grace, which motivates us to be ruled more and more by love and less by the movements of fear. As life and the work of loving our family tests us, love and trust develop and grow stronger. When we remain faithful even in disappointment, loss, and sorrow, we face the ultimate test. In all these situations, love remains the heart of a mother's calling.

The Word of God teaches us not to be afraid of our calling (Luke 1:30; Deut 31:8), nor of any failure but the ruin of our spirits (Luke 12:4). Scripture also uses the words *do not be afraid* at the two pivotal points in the life of Christ, his birth and his resurrection. At his birth, the angels told the shepherds, "Do not fear," and at the tomb of the risen Lord, those to whom he revealed himself were told not to be afraid (Luke 2:10; Matt 28:5). This reveals that our confidence is in Christ, because of his coming and his triumph over death. It is even a source of boldness, of which St. Paul reminds us (2 Cor 3:12; Heb 4:16). Further, the psalms are filled with injunctions against fear. We read, for example:

> Many are rising against me;
> many are saying to me,
>   "There is no help for you in God."
> But you, O LORD, are a shield around me,
>   my glory, and the one who lifts up my head....
>   The LORD sustains me,
> I am not afraid of ten thousands of people....
> Rise up, O LORD!
>   Deliver me, O my God. (Ps 3:1–3, 5–8)

This cry is answered, "Thus says the LORD who made you, who formed you in the womb and will help you; Do not fear, O Jacob my servant, Jeshurun whom I have chosen" (Isa 44:2).

These readings and many others present a Christian logic for overcoming fear. Trust alone enables us to experience love as a reality greater than all the objects of our fear combined. Our true security lies, paradoxically, not in our ability to protect ourselves from harm, but in our creaturely vulnerability itself. When we are honest about our vulnerability, we are in a situation to recognize our need for God and come to depend not on ourselves but on God. For mothers, our path to greater trust and love lies within our vocation to love in the family setting. It is thus deeply tied to the social aspect of human nature, to the inexorable linkages between human beings. We grow and thrive through our connectedness.

THE HUMAN COMMUNITY AND THE NOTION OF "ORGANIC CHARITY"

There would be little or no social cohesion without intentionality and choice. How we relate to other people and chose our friends not only forms the body of society, but it builds us individually. Sociologists have described family as the foundational cell of society. Beyond the family, we are linked to other families through shared interests that allow us to express our social nature. It is not simply that we live side by side. We intentionally share common interests and goals, or common moral or religious commitments with different groups. For example, the shared interest of quality education among parents whose children attend the same school. Each of us participates in formal and informal institutions, which constitute civil society. Another example of intentional association is government, the social contract that bundles our shared interests and holds elected leaders accountable to meeting specific needs of the whole.

Despite the complexity of society, all of our associations are based on a prior, physical connection within our family of origin. If we trace the link that binds community, it begins with mother and child, with the connection between them through the umbilical cord. This is our organic, primordial "social" experience. It is interesting to note that our most basic connection is based on acceptance rather than choice. It is based on trust and openness to the unknown. The umbilical chord symbolizes an organic interdependence that is the first experience of every human person. While the details of childbirth are often cleaned up and forgotten, almost with a sense of shame, the fact remains that the earliest existence of each and every human being is of a lifeline of food and oxygen tied to another human being. Is there not a memory in our bodies of this interpersonal link? Mothers certainly feel linked to their children and vice versa in the first years of life and beyond. Throughout our growing-up years, we are taught to strive for independence and self-sufficiency. Yet human connectedness and interdependence is embedded deep within us, written in our DNA, and impressed upon our psyches. Mothers know, even over the years, that this connection holds fast. It is not uncommon for mothers of grown children to speak of them with the same tender sense of connection and intimacy that characterized their love for that son or daughter as a child.

There are other organic links between us. In Scripture, Jesus quotes Genesis to instruct his followers on marriage, saying, a man will leave his family and cling to his wife: "'And the two shall become one flesh.' So they are no longer two but one flesh. Therefore what God has joined together, let no one separate" (Mark 10:8–9). St. Paul commented further on this unity of flesh in his letter on the Christian household, insisting that a man should love his wife as he does his own flesh. Paul also enjoins a mutuality of love and respect between husband and wife based on physical, personal, and spiritual union (Eph 5:21, 28 ff). The unity of "one flesh" is the antecedent of the creation and birth of a child. Out of the intention by two lovers to begin a family, a new flesh is creatively given out of the "one flesh" of the parents. This is the original blueprint of love into which a child would be conceived and born.

While love is certainly not always present when a child is conceived, it remains the goodness that God originally desired and planned: that each of us be born into the society of love between a man and a woman, freely and intentionally chosen. Through grace, love is meant to thrive in the core of our family relationships, a love displayed through flesh and blood—a growing, organic love that is symbol and presence of the love of God in the Trinity. What a mistake to think we must put family aside to live spiritual lives! The very love God intends when he forms us as human beings resides in the intimacy and sacred ground of family. If we are unconvinced, we should remember that Jesus himself spent some thirty years working and living in the family and Galilean community before he manifested himself publicly as teacher and Messiah.

"Organic charity" is simply another way of stating Thomas Aquinas's famous principle: grace builds on nature. It describes the truth that God works right here, right now, in the very stuff of our daily lives: mealtimes and bedtimes, bodies, deadlines, illnesses, baseball games, jobs gained and careers lost, joys as well as disappointments. It is the love God calls us to in family life, a love we have to work at just as we must in any other relationship we care about. We may pretend that love between family members is easy because of the biological connection we share. On the other hand, we may think our family is too dysfunctional to receive grace. But the love at work in family goes far beyond instinct and reaches deep into our dysfunctional patterns. On a daily basis, the Holy Spirit breathes into our human reality. Because it is a work of the Spirit, we can love each other in godly ways. This is the sacramental nature of family life. If we identify the spiritual lessons inherent in family life, we can grow into this continuous sacrament so that each family becomes a visible sign of God's invisible love and life.

LESSONS IN THE SCHOOL OF LOVE

Family is a school of spiritual lessons that train us in organic charity. Mothers set the tone and have a large say in the "curriculum" of this school. We can learn most from sharing the wisdom of our mothers and grandmothers, trusted friends, and our own intuition. We may also learn from a few proven professionals. Most of all, the Spirit assists us. Some of the lessons at the heart of organic charity follow.

Lesson One Is the Body

The body teaches lesson one. The woman risks more and gives more when a couple decides to start a family. Her intentionality in this, therefore, is crucial. We assume that, in a healthy sexual relationship, freedom and intentionality are present. In becoming mothers, women need to have at least the same freedom and intentionality in order to fully accept the challenge.

The body is a permanent aspect of family life. It begins with the intimacy of erotic love, the unity of flesh between a husband and wife spoken of by Jesus and St. Paul, a mutual, physical love. In this physical relationship, a woman has not only a passive role, but also an active one to seek out her husband, to accept his love, and to share her own. Ideally, her freedom to give herself to another is the link between the sensual love of a wife and the heroic love of a mother. She bears greater responsibility out of the couple's joint decision to become parents.

Family starts in the body of a pregnant woman, who gives decisively and generously from the day she assents to become a mother. Instinct is only the beginning, as she is challenged again and again to love in deed and not just in word. A mother utters a prolonged "yes" by her nine-month willingness to give her body to nurture and form her child until the time of birth. God fits us for the challenges of being pregnant and breathes into us the Holy Spirit to live out such generosity. In a woman's receptive love for the child still in her womb, yet to come, she is on her way to experiencing a new way of loving that is rooted in the feminine being. In utero, a baby takes up a specific amount of space within the body and needs nourishment through the mother's food. Because of the intense physicality of pregnancy, labor, and birth, women grow in their intuitive awareness of the importance of the body.

After birth comes the enormous commitment to care for and console our child in a thousand different ways. This care reinforces the embodied aspect of our nature. A mother and anyone else who cares for a new baby introduce the child to the sensory world: color and light, song and speech, lips and embraces; the warm scents of milk and home, the taste of the mother's body, and the touch of loving hands. All mediate to the child a cherishing love through the body. Such physical intimacy also reminds a mother of her own bodily self. In a world that splits mind and body, we are forced to hold together daily the confounding mystery that we are a unified "spirit body." One of the primary ways this is brought home to us is through touch.

The hallmark of organic charity is touch. There is no charity apart from the body. A short inventory of the gospel reveals that Jesus was always reaching out to touch those with whom he interacted. He healed from the first moment of his public ministry. He rebuked evil with his voice, but he healed people with his hands. In the first chapter of Mark, we read that Peter's mother-in-law was sick with a fever, and Jesus "came and *took her by the hand and lifted her up*" and she was cured (Mark 1:31). Jesus stayed in her home, curing those who gathered in great numbers. "A leper came to him begging him, and kneeling he said to him, 'If you choose, you can make me clean.' Moved with pity, Jesus stretched out his hand *and touched him* and said to him, 'I do choose. Be made clean!' Immediately the leprosy left him, and he was made clean (Mark 1:40–42). Jesus' power went out from him when the woman with the hemorrhage *touched him*, desiring to be healed. He raised the daughter of Jairus from the dead, *taking her by the hand* and commanding her to get up (Luke 8).

The physical nourishing of nursing is where touch begins. It is closely tied to the spiritual and psychological building up of the babe's sense of safety, intimacy, and warmth. "Nature has designed labor, birth, and the postpartum period as a crucial time to maximize touch. This imprints well-being."[1]

The first days and weeks after our child is born are like the first day of a revolution. When a revolution happens, there is a shift in power, and a new kind of authority begins to organize the life of a community. When a woman becomes a mother, a new power arises within her. This new regime pushes toward a reorganization of her psyche and self that allows her to express her deepest tendencies as a feminine self. The energy she possesses intrinsically emerges to become an active force in the world. This force is essentially a drive to create and preserve life out of the substance of her very body and person. This same energy is with us throughout our lives as mothers. The time we spend with our child early on is a continuation of the creative power operative in the womb, only now it is a psychological and interpersonal reality that forms our children and us.

A baby has only just left the near-perfectly regulated atmosphere of the hushed and darkened womb, and is still learning to breathe, to know and be known. What a transition! It is no wonder that a newborn needs so much care. As we preoccupy ourselves with his or her physical care, our touch meets spiritual and psychological needs. Touch is the primary medium of communication, and even speech is a language of vibration and tactile sensation in a pre-reasoning mode. Mothers experience a propensity to sing, to babble silly things, to whisper, to play. Visual interaction is also important. We place our faces close to our baby and toys as well, so he or she can see. The baby is becoming aware of its own embodied nature through this mothering. The interaction between a mothering person and a child speaks volumes of the goodness of creation, the graciousness of God who loves us as whole beings, as body-soul beings.

In response to a mother's communicative touch, a child will respond as he or she grows and will learn to clearly express love and appreciation for the beauty and the value of others: when the small hand reaches up to caress your face or to reach out and hold you tight; when the little face comes close to yours to share a secret or a smile; when you hear those first words of love, of naming, *Mama, Dada*. These are the lessons of touch that come to us through our children and mark us with an experience of God's care. But the small child must learn such respectful, free expression by first receiving it.

Lesson Two Is Discipline

We require discipline to organize our lives. The changes occur at the deeper levels of self as well as at the mundane levels of adapting to our lifestyle as mothers, an ongoing challenge throughout a mother's long career. It is helpful to become aware of the dynamic of these changes so that we can embrace ourselves as mothers and thrive in new ways.

In spiritual jargon, this discipline is called *asceticism*. The word is derived from the Greek, meaning to train through exercises. Using the words of spirituality may seem jarring, but it helps us to be honest about what really happens to us and to be intentional about how we deal with it. "As much as any religious order, the very essence of mothering is a discipline that can teach us about ourselves and God, a discipline that is as rigorous as any other spiritual path."[2] Training is an intentional form of exercise undertaken for a specific purpose. As mothers, all we do is part of our spiritual undertaking, as we order our lives toward family for the sake of love. The two great commandments—love the Lord your God and love your neighbor—come together in an organic way as we live out the responsibilities of our calling. We must experience renunciation daily, loving others beyond self, beyond our vulnerability, accepting the ties that bind, with open arms to community. Often we are surprised by the degree of discipline involved, a likely result of our romanticized notions of motherhood. Being honest about the asceticism helps us to both accept the sacrifices we make graciously and, just as important, to avoid excess.

Lesson Three Is Mercy

Family life has its particular pitfalls. We tend to take each other for granted, to show our true colors: the good, the bad, the ugly. Conflict is part of family life, but how we respond to each other in daily life is the raw material of mercy. St. John wrote that if we think we love the invisible God but do not love our neighbor, whom we can see, then we are liars. Wendy Wright offers a commentary on this need to live in peace with those closest to us. She reports that, in a survey of Catholic lay ministers who minister to families, the participants held that forgiveness is the key spiritual dynamic of family life.[3] In his discussion about the retreat of St. Ignatius, G. Aschenbrenner speaks of love as a dynamic, not static reality: a development "worked in a human heart by God's love."[4] Aschenbrenner shows that the kind of peace we desire to experience in family life is something that is "worked" in our hearts by God. What allows that holy work to go forward, however, is mercy and the willingness to forgive one another. One of the most meaningful things a mother or father can do, after a long day, when the time for prayer before bed comes, is to admit to a child his or her own failings. When we know, and we know our child knows, that we have lost control in anger or acted selfishly, nothing deflates conflict and welcomes in peace better than asking forgiveness. God is the instigator, the one directing the transformation of our hearts to love God and one another.

Lesson Four Is Fellowship

Psalm 33 exclaims, "How very good and pleasant it is when kindred live together in unity." This psalm, traditionally called *Ecce Quam Bonum* from its opening words in Latin, is customarily used in monastic orders at the time of taking vows. It expresses the commitment a candidate for religious life makes to his or her community or religious family. Fellowship is at the heart of the love commitment, through which the religious will live out his or her calling and become holy. This same dynamic is operative in family life, the place of God's blessing described in this psalm.

The psalmist uses the words *good, pleasant,* and *precious* to describe a family living in a way that fosters unity. It is like the welcome and meal offered to a guest in hospitality. This is refreshing and life-giving to both giver and receiver. Fellowship in our family life welcomes others and welcomes God like a beloved guest. When we strive to live in unity, the water of grace is upon us like the droplets of dew on grass. However, it is important to remember that God's blessing does not depend on our success, on whether or not we can achieve our own idea of "harmony" in the household. Nor does it depend on the absence of conflict. Instead, God's blessing depends on our openness to the dynamic development of his work in our hearts to bring us closer together in the midst of the daily need for forgiveness as we bear with one another patiently. The unity spoken of in this psalm means we share the same vision for our life together; namely, that it is rooted in love and mutual forgiveness. We can stop waiting for the day when our spouse changes his or her annoying behavior or the moment when our child turns into a model of obedience. We need not expect that we ourselves will never again act in anger or do things we are later ashamed of. These false expectations will only cause us to give up early. Speaking of Jesus' breathing the Holy Spirit into the early Church, Wendy Wright wrote, "Through mutual forgiveness they would become a genuine community, not of isolated individuals coexisting in a state of armed truce but a communion that shares one life because each member is animated by the vital energy of the Spirit."[5] The Spirit breathes into us the life of love that is at the heart of a united family.

Lesson Five Is Discernment

Family life is the building block of the Church. As families, we live the call of Christ to love one another in a daily, uninterrupted fashion. How do we become aware of the action of the Spirit? St. Ignatius offered the examination of conscience, what Aschenbrenner calls the "consciousness examen," which is a way of examining what forces are at work in us during a given day or other period of time. This practice leads to growing awareness of the breath of God's Spirit in the concrete and real situations of our lives. As we pay attention to these different movements of the Spirit, we enter with purpose into that dynamic work which God is doing in our hearts. This allows us to make progress toward greater and greater spiritual freedom. The steps of this practice are listed in the Encounter and Practice exercises at the end of this chapter.

Discernment is nothing less than coming to see God at work in my own life. We often presume God is present only under certain conditions. Discernment gives us the tools to sift through *all* our experience and articulate for ourselves where God is leading. This helps us to discover our direction and purpose in the context of our particular work and vocation.

How we live together as family affects the society in which we live. Every healthy family is a healthy cell in the body of a community. Mothers set the tone for family life. We are at the front lines of all that goes on in a home, not because we do all the work of running a home personally—for many today, thankfully, have help. It is rather part of the nature of our calling to set the tone, to foster life in the body and the life of the spirit. Our task is to become more and more open to grace, so that we may grow in love and cast out fear.

ENCOUNTER AND PRACTICE

Encounter

The five steps of the examen can be done while walking or at rest. One or another of the steps may be dwelt on at length. It is especially helpful to give thanks, for example, when feeling out of sorts or restless.

1. *Thanksgiving.* We begin by acknowledging that God is present and active in our lives. This combats our bias toward believing God is far off and inaccessible. St. Paul tells us to approach the very throne of God with confidence. In this first movement, our spirit opens to a God who is present here and now, who desires to lead us through this day inspired by his own Spirit. We give thanks for this presence and loving action. We give thanks for anything that comes up: for a sunny weekend, for reconciliation with a family member. We allow our hearts to see and become more conscious of how much we are loved, how much we've been given.

2. *Enlightenment from Above.* The other side of gratitude is disappointment. We feel disappointment when we experience our own failures and those of others. Many times discord is born of our refusal to see where we are wrong and how we fail to love. We blame others and insist we are right. At this step we ask God to give us light so that we may know what we are holding back in fear, unwilling to cooperate with the work of the Spirit. What hinders growth and stifles joy? How is family unity being thwarted?

3. *Examination of Life*: Scripture says that the just man falls seven times a day, meaning that the just man is aware of his fall while the unjust is completely unaware. In this step, we look at the last day or the last half-day. We seek self-awareness and humble recognition of how we have failed one another in love. This is the first step toward unity, because it is the first step toward forgiveness. If we are not aware we have hurt another person, how can we possibly seek forgiveness? It is within the deeply personal realm of conscience that this step takes place and it is truly sacred ground. Before God, we are who we are.

4. *Confession and Forgiveness*. This is a moment not of shame but of sorrow at our failings in love—to people whom we love, such as our spouse, our children, our parents, our friends—to God, and, yes, even to ourselves. Asking God's forgiveness is all about letting our defenses down so that we may be vulnerable enough to love. Again, Wright says, "To disarm the heart is the work of a lifetime"[6] In the act of confessing and then asking forgiveness, we allow grace to disarm our defenses, absolve our guilt, and give us a new start to love in greater freedom. The dynamic of this step is to separate the false self from the true. Paradoxically, guilty feelings are dissolved by this practice. Gratitude displaces guilt because it makes us gradually more conscious of how immeasurably more powerful is God's mercy and compassion for us than any wrongdoing on our part.

Practice

5. *Resolution to Action*. When prayer is divorced from action it is sterile and empty. It can even make us stumble into self-righteous pride. In the fifth step of the examen, we place ourselves at the dis-

posal of the Holy Spirit. We ask God to help to counter those things already identified, the sins that hold us back and thwart charity. Each of us discovers his or her own particular practice under the inspiration of the Holy Spirit through this step. It requires a listening heart and ready hands to do the works God has in store for each. This is a moment of intimate dialogue with God who makes known to us, not how to save the world, but how to take the next step forward. We invite the Spirit to breathe into us the breath of new life (Gen 1:7), so we can live to love God, abide in love, and play our part in the work of the Holy Spirit to build up the kingdom of heaven.

CHAPTER FIVE

Filled with Compassion

Inspired Parenting for Today

> "While he was still far off, his father saw him and was filled with compassion; he ran and put his arms around him and kissed him."
>
> Luke 15:20

Each of us brings to parenting our own experiences growing up, the negative and the positive, the blessings and maybe a curse or two. We also face new problems that our parents and grandparents did not know. Roles are not as clearly defined as they once were, and women and men both struggle with parenting in our fast-moving age. Kate Figes captures our situation well: "We live in stirring, exciting times, when the rules within relationships are more fluid and unconventional than ever and are being defined by the individuals involved rather than by social constraint."[1] This can be a double-edged sword. Clearly defined roles provide security, and their absence can cause unease. Like water that has lost its tranquil surface, we may become unsettled and stressed. Yet the fluid nature of relationships can also create new possibilities. We can be more honest about problems formerly ignored or denied, and more open to new ways of relating to one another. Forced out of our comfort zone, we may even find that the very difficulties we face become an impetus toward growth. Where do we look for inspiration in this situation?

In earlier chapters, we have found inspiration in Scripture in Sarah, Mary, and Elizabeth. These women received their vocation to motherhood and to participate in God's plan. Yet there is a central question for mothers we have not yet addressed; that is, the role of fathers. This will be our focal point as we discuss the changes in parenting today and insights from the parable of the Prodigal Son.

As we seek for guidance in family relationships in our time and place, God is calling us to go deeper, discovering new insights within our old institutions and traditions. Our search is fundamentally a process of discernment in which we look for that which helps us grow and find newness of life. For Christians, this discernment implies the work of the eternal Spirit, whose breathing in and out vivifies the people of God with God's own life, light, and power. Inspiration does not refer to ideas and musings that make us feel good for a time, but have no staying power. It carries the connotation of breath: the very respiration we depend upon to keep living. Metaphorically speaking, inspiration keeps us alive spiritually and emotionally. It enables us to live our routine lives with imagination and hope, passion and conviction. Through the process of discernment, we root out all that traps the spirit, kills the imagination, and hinders healthy human relationships.

We find the Spirit's inspiration in primarily two places: in Scripture, coupled with prayer in the process of discernment, and in the life of the Church; that is, in dialogue with the lived experience of God's people. We now turn to these sources for inspiration about the role of fathers in family life.

THE IDEAL OF MUTUALITY

There are some positive developments in the relationship between the sexes within families. Since most women in the United States have careers or work outside the home, parents of small children have had to come to terms with the fact that men as well as women have an important role to play in the care of children and the home. Statistically, women still do the majority of childcare and housework. Still, the value of partnership and mutuality in raising children has grown. In this setting, men have the opportunity to discover their own ways of loving and nurturing, as well as disciplining and teaching children. Another positive development is that the loosening of stringent role divisions can help men and women to be less exclusive and possessive of their respective duties. The marriage relationship and parenting are a decidedly joint venture. By sharing their responsibilities, work, and insights with each other, men and women can develop a stronger relationship and empathize with one another. It is harder to take the other person for granted when you have walked a mile in her slippers at the 2:00 a.m. diapering-and-feeding time.

Contrast this with a home where one or both parents work many hours outside the home, with little time for contact with children. Does this not pose a risk of alienation from parenting as a vocation? While we may think of this as deprivation for children (they are not with the parent), children are resilient. Consider instead that it is parents who miss the chance to know the graces of their vocation, the spiritual and personal insights, the struggles but also the joys.

Sharing the responsibility of raising children can foster balance in family life and a humanization of our individual lives. This sharing requires that men and women let go of their grip on traditional roles so that they can accept together the challenges and gifts that each experiences differently, and so can better empathize with the other. What makes the difference is mutuality and shared responsibility, as well as the rewards in family life and work. It is very difficult, however, to prioritize home life in our economy-driven culture.

We live in a workaholic culture. Working parents can be so taken up by their jobs that they suffer amnesia about the need to build relationships, enjoy those bonds, and take time for Sabbath rest. We also live in a consumer culture. The parent who stays home with children may become overly obsessed with concern for the "perfect" development of the children, or worse, the perfect coordination of the interior decoration scheme. Yet we cannot purchase or orchestrate the fulfillment of our children's potential. Mothers and children especially are considered a lucrative market audience, while men are perhaps more vulnerable to the temptation to overwork. In either case, parents can be chronically distracted from a shared family life by the pressure to conform to the economic ideal of family life. The sharing of roles can be a corrective, so that men and women help each other.

Sometimes this mutuality will be a sharing of gifted moments, such as the joy of being present when a child utters his or her first words or learns to do something for the first time. This helps prevent the absent parent from totally missing the delight of family life. At other times the mutuality will be a sharing in the cross, the acceptance of the responsibility of discipline and education, and all the many unexpected difficulties and challenges of raising children. Men and women each bring particular gifts and ways of relating that enrich the family dynamic. Mutuality helps them share these differences more effectively.

This giving and sharing is also an important dynamic for spiritual freedom. It makes us humble enough to learn from each other, but also more aware of our own strengths. When we are able to learn from each other, we are in a better position to let go of unhealthy behavior that stifles loving family relationships. "We cannot expect to maintain the monopoly on motherhood simply because we create and give birth to our children."[2] Nor can men any longer have a monopoly on the world of work and career beyond the home.

Authentic Christian spirituality always involves a gradual growth in freedom. For those who are called to grow closer to God in the context of family life, traditionally separate roles for men and women have not always fostered the kind of freedom and the mutual sharing of life that Christ calls us to. For, "to be real, spirituality must empower."[3] In this sense, marriage and parenting have remained partly unredeemed. Christians have so neatly internalized the sin of our "first parents"—and the rift between the sexes central to that story—that we have not yet allowed the power of the gospels to sufficiently heal us.

The entrance of sin into God's creation is a tragedy men and women share. Adam and Eve ate together what was forbidden, and together they shared in the consequences, each accepting a consequence related to their particular giftedness. Adam's work became sweat and toil, while Eve's life-giving gift in bearing children became dangerous and painful. Because sin originated in the context of the love relationship between men and women, it may be precisely here that human beings experience the most resistance to conversion.

In the gospels, however, Jesus calls men and women to live, not as if still trapped in sin, but as children of God. In Mark 19:3–9, the Pharisees ask him if a man can divorce his wife "for any cause." Jesus tells them to go back to the beginning, to Genesis before the fall: "The two shall become one flesh." Jesus even explains that the Law of Moses was not the ideal for his followers, saying, "It was because you are so hard-hearted that Moses allowed you to divorce your wives, but from the beginning it was not so." When his disciples question him further about this—exasperated at the notion that men could not divorce their wives—Jesus responds calmly that such a love and commitment were a gift: "Not everyone can accept this teaching, but only those to whom it is given." Jesus understands the challenge of mutuality. The ideal for him is a shared life, "one flesh," that will allow each to know and respect the truth of the other.

We are living at a time when men and women can embrace the facets of their respective vocations more freely and richly with the help of the Holy Spirit. Yet there is also contention over this. The ideal of "one flesh" and the fulfillment of this passage are hindered partly by a perception of fatherhood, and of men in general.

Today, the father image is wounded. We live within a patriarchal society and culture, which carries over into many institutions, including Christian Churches. Feminism has made us more aware of sexism and gender-based abuses of power. In some parts of the world, abuse and oppression of women are still widespread. This can cast a shadow over men and fathers, as if to equate maleness, and especially fatherhood, with oppression. It can be difficult to find inspiration in fatherhood with this often-invisible weight upon the shoulders of men and families. We acknowledge this inherited cultural backdrop as we address the father's role in the family.

In all the gospels, Jesus takes great care to describe the most important relationship of his life, the one he had with God, whom he called "Father." Jesus' view of the Father can help us restore beauty and honor to our notion of fatherhood. We undertake this not as an academic exercise, but as a personal search for healing the marred aspects of our father-image. Who is God the Father, and how can this Father inspire a Christian father in the care of his own children and family? To do this, we have to imagine something that transcends the culturally biased notions of men and fathers described above. We have to imagine the Father as Jesus presents him.

GOD AS FATHER: LIBERATOR AND GIVER OF GOOD THINGS

St. Paul invokes God as the Father from whom earthly fatherhood takes its name. This is our rationale for rooting Christian fatherhood in God and not in a simple social convention. Next, we should realize that Jesus called God Father in the first place to help us understand the relationship he had with God. Because of his relationship, we would have the chance to become God's children through our likeness to and union with Christ. The qualities we associate with fatherhood—such as authority, generative power, providence, protection, and so on—are exemplified by other metaphors in Scripture: King, Parent, Mother, Creator, or Rock of Refuge. But it is only by calling God "Our Father" in Jesus that we can become privileged sons and daughters, with the rights of inheritance in Christ. We are transformed from lost, exiled sinners into children of God.[4]

The misrepresentation of God as a literal father has gotten us into trouble. It has at times caused a focus on authority and fear-based obedience to the detriment of mercy and unconditional love. Revisiting God the Father as Jesus presents him—and keeping this in tension with other images, metaphors, and personifications of God in Scripture—helps us grow out of an image of the Father as unreasonable, authoritarian, and even forgetful of human beings. One important name for God that has served the pastoral needs of people today is that of Liberator.

God as Liberator evokes the exodus story of Moses, who freed Israel from slavery. It was God who heard the cries of his people and took notice. The God of Moses is a model for all the liberations by which people seek to be free of sin and death in the name of God. Today, liberation dominates the social and religious landscape because people are enslaved in so many new ways. The search for liberation is not simply a fad or the vain pursuit of selfish achievement. On the contrary, here it refers to a timeless symptom of humankind's desperate need for God, shared by all, whether consciously or not, in the face of sin. When we hold the image of God as Liberator together with God the Father, we see a clearer picture of the kind of God Jesus wanted us to imagine, a Father who established and continues to honor the total freedom of his children. This freedom will be highlighted in our discussion of the parable below. It is central to the way God acts as Father toward his sons and daughters.

This freedom, the first gift of God the Father, also helps us understand the authority of God *as* Father. By God's design, that authority is mysteriously open, even contingent, for the sake of human freedom. God gives us many gifts and opportunities, but allows us to choose how to live. The Father refrains from exercising absolute power over his children. Instead, God makes freedom the mother of authentic love, and the hallmark of the divine relationship with each person. God speaks to us, makes himself known, and asks us to steward the earth and our own lives wisely. But it is ours to decide.[5]

Another image closely related to the fatherhood of God is that of Giver of Gifts. Jesus shows us this giving Father when he chides the disciples for their lack of faith. They have asked Jesus to teach them how to pray. He teaches them to pray calling God "father" and then asks, "Is there anyone among you, who, if your child asks for a fish, will give a snake instead of a fish? Or if the child asks for an egg, will give a scorpion? If you then, who are evil, know how to give good gifts to your children, how much more will the heavenly Father give the Holy Spirit to those who ask him!" (Luke 11:11–13) In Matthew 7:11, the same passage promises "good things."

Jesus describes the basic attitude of fatherhood as "giving good things" to his children who ask. Any father would want to provide sustenance—fish, an egg, a loaf of bread. Fatherhood has this aspect of generous giving, akin to nurturance. But Jesus asks us to imagine the Father's goodness and generosity as greater still, and the Father's love as a reality far beyond the love parents have for children. "How much more will your Father in heaven give to those who ask?" In that small query, Jesus points to the very difference between the human and the divine. This Father desires to give far more than any parent could.

Jesus also expresses his relationship to the Father as one of familiar intimacy. In these passages, Jesus calls God *Abba*, an expression akin to "Dad" (Mark 14:36; Gal 4:6). The Father is not a distant figure of power, but one whom the Son knows well (John 14:8–14).

How can we reconcile this generous Father with the image of God that seems to prevail culturally, that of an unforgiving perfectionist, unsympathetic to human suffering? It seems quite normal to look at natural disasters, birth defects, social injustice, and the countless ills of our world and to blame God, as if God would order such events purposely to test humanity. This would make God into a megalomaniac who has infinite power yet refuses to save humanity from suffering and death. However, this is clearly not the Father Jesus has revealed to us.

PARENTAL POWER

The gospels paint a picture of the Father as giving good things. We may call this act "nurturing" for women and "providing" for fathers; each expresses the love of sharing good things in different ways at different times. A mother can be both provider and nurturer. A father can also take part in both. Through the offering of material and spiritual gifts, we prove or give evidence of our love. The gift carries, or at least should, this affirming message of love. Absent this love, the gift is literally worthless. Whatever power we have "over" our children, our God-given authority is meant to be at the service of love. Our ability to provide for them in a myriad ways—to teach, nourish, and keep them under our care—makes us like the Father, as we foster their growth into free and healthy adults. Is this example of the Father who gives "good things" to his children not an inspiration to all fathers as well as mothers? Is it not an inspiration to generosity of time and love—of themselves—of which the gift is but a sign? Parental authority, which will be addressed further in the parable of the Prodigal Son below, is an exercise of power at the service of love. This truth requires the renunciation of certain kinds of power in imitation of God the Father.

Joan Chittister quotes Rollo May's description of five kinds of power: exploitative, competitive, manipulative, integrative, and nurturing.[6] She critiques the first three forms of power and makes the claim that the very purpose of having power is to empower others.

Yet today we think of power in general as a good thing. Hesitating to use what power we have, or, even more incomprehensible, renouncing power, would be considered a sign of weakness. It could cause us to fail, to become impoverished, or even to get sick and die. Only a naive person would try to make it in today's world without competing, manipulating, and even exploiting others "when necessary." Those who have a greater share of the power pie are allowed and expected to use the means required to keep and grow their power. These cultural assumptions, however, are antithetical to the image of God as the Father as Jesus portrayed him. Especially for men, these forms of power can be destructive when they are quietly accepted as a form of virtue. While none of us is free from resorting to these kinds of power from time to time, any more than we are free of sin, what is being critiqued here is their harmful idealization as virtue. We then become quite blind to their insidious dynamic in our lives.

The gospel contains a model for exercising power that reflects the Father's love and his calling us to live inspired by the values of the kingdom of heaven. This model is given to us in the Parable of the Prodigal Son. This is an especially inspired model for fathers who wish to imitate the generous love of the Father as they exercise their parental authority.

The way in which men use their power and influence is extremely important for the family and health of society. The wider social norms for the use of power are rooted in the family. One has only to study the forms of familial authority in the Middle East and their social repercussions for women and children to see this connection. However, even given the more extreme patriarchal forms of power in place during Jesus' lifetime, Jesus did not hesitate to proclaim a different kind of power and a new rationale for the use of authority. It is to this example we now turn.

POWER AS MERCY: THE PRODIGAL SON

Jesus begins his story of the Prodigal Son: "There was a man who had two sons..." (Luke 15:11–3). Imagine two talented, handsome, young men, blessed with material abundance and filled with a youthful lust for life. They are ready to tackle any challenge with a no-holes-barred, can-do attitude. The boys have all the potential for a brilliant future. Then one day, the younger son suddenly asks for his portion of the inheritance, a request that was equivalent to treating his father like one already dead. In a few short days, everything changes for this family. The youth cannot contain his wanderlust and refuses to be confined on his father's estate. He leaves for a "distant land," and like a wild-eyed adventurer, he strikes out and doesn't look back. He travels far and wide and enjoys all that life has to offer. He leaves no appetite unappeased. Oblivious and self-satisfied, he stays away for years. Meanwhile, his departure has been like a death in the family. The son becomes a distant memory and, for his father, an aching sorrow.

One day, however, the son's happiness comes to an end. His money runs out, and he is cursed with bad luck. A famine strikes the land where he is living and he becomes extremely poor. All his squandering and devouring of "the father's property with prostitutes" and "dissolute" living has left him hitting bottom. He has become so desperate that he works tending the swine, unclean animals, revolting and disgraceful to him and his people.

At this low ebb, the young man begins to reflect. In an early example of a Christian examination of conscience, the young man "came to himself," or he came to his senses, a phrase used to show the moment of conversion. An example of this graced moment has happened before, in the history of Israel: "For I know that they will not obey me, for they are a stiff-necked people. But in the land of their exile they will come to themselves" (Bar 2:30). "Stiff-necked" describes well the interior attitude of this man in his youth, a stubborn, rigid attitude that made him gradually lose a sense of himself. His life so far was a long chain of decisions and actions that expressed his own wild willfulness, but not his true self. Now, in a moment of truth, he suddenly sees the devastating results of his selfish behavior. He is alone and starving, in "exile." Suffering becomes the catalyst for clarity, and all at once he realizes that he has traveled many years in the wrong direction! He is lost like the sheep that wanders away, like the coin that is forgotten in a dirty corner. The prodigal son is struck to the depths of his heart: I am utterly abandoned!

In hunger and desperation, he cries out to himself, "I will get up and go to my father and I will say to him, 'Father, I have sinned against heaven and before you; I am no longer worthy to be called your son; treat me like one of your hired hands'" (Luke 15:18). This is the most important decision of his life. It is the moment he turns from falsehood to truth, expressed in the words, "he came to himself."

While the young man is turning away from his despair, the father has been vigilant, on the lookout, always hoping to one day see his son again. Father and son, each carrying his own sorrow alone, are about to reconcile. One day, the father sees his son coming from far off. Like one who has rehearsed this many times, he runs to meet his son. Overjoyed, he embraces him. He seems not to hear his son's own rehearsed repentance. Instead, he calls out for the servants: Bring the best garments to clothe my son! Place a ring on his finger! Kill the fatted calf! Let us all be glad and rejoice, for my son is here! He "was dead and has come to life; he was lost and has been found" (Luke 15:32).

Any father, any parent, will resonate with this image. Who can forget his or her child? Neither mother nor father! Even after being betrayed and failed, the father knows who his son is and longs for his return. When the rest of the family arrives on the scene, we can imagine the mother is overjoyed. However, the older brother refuses to hear any of this. The older brother is furious with his father: Your other son hardly has the right to be treated as a hired hand, yet you feed and clothe him, embrace him, shower him with the best that money can buy. The elder son is beside himself with anger at this seeming injustice. The answer the father gives to this faithful son, however, shows what it means to be one with the Father as he shows by this plea: You are with me always, but this is your brother returned, and we must celebrate.

MISERICORDIA

Our reading of this parable presents the love of the father at the center of family life. It is also a reference point for cultural critique. This is the Father's way of loving that is to inspire all fathers. Just as mothers share of the insight of their experience in mothering through pregnancy, birth, and infancy, so fathers have a grace to share. It is mercy. It is empowerment. It is being at the service of the family through love and being willing to do anything so that not one of those the Father has given them will be lost (John 17:12).

There are several ways the parable gives an insight into the father's role in family life. First, the father does not exercise power over his child that would be due him under the law, but instead he displays the most astounding virtues of generosity and an existential respect for his child's freedom. This must have caused consternation in Jesus' audience of Pharisees and religious leaders. The father's actions seemed unfair and unreasonable. Once he left, the vagabond son deserved to be as one dead to his father and all his kin, disgraced and disowned. The elder son who dutifully stayed with his father should have been rewarded. Instead, the story barely mentions him until the end, and then the father doesn't listen to what seemed like a just complaint. Jesus' parable undermines the strict justice and rules of patriarchy that would have dictated that the elder son inherit everything upon the father's death. Jesus thus transcends the cultural norms of his day to demonstrate how God relates to us as Father. Mercy—in the Spanish, *misericordia*—expresses that the father acts from the heart (*corde*), and that the heart is the Father's response to misery (*miseria*) or want. The Father keeps watch for our free decision to seek God, so that he may give his heart to us in our need.

There is a powerful love at work here that is the backdrop for the mystery of salvation. It reaffirms our earlier theme: the inexplicable divine decree that God's creatures would be free. The prodigal son must choose for himself to remain in the family business or leave; to follow the ways and traditions of his family or break away; to spend time in the company of his brothers, sisters, mother and father, or go his own way. Each of us must make our own choice.

If God shows a simple, even humble, respect for human freedom, as parents we share this kind of love. We teach our children to gradually take greater responsibility for themselves as they grow into adulthood, until they no longer need us. Loving this way is filled with a strange apprehension for our children, but it is also filled with the joy of seeing them experience life for themselves and grow into a confident sense of self. In fact, this joy is the whole point of the story.

Notice that Luke presents the Parable of the Prodigal Son immediately after two other parables that reflect a similar theme: the shepherd who leaves behind all ninety-nine sheep to go and look for the one lost sheep, and the woman who turns her home upside down searching for a lost coin. After each parable Jesus delivers the punch line: there is more joy in heaven over one lost sinner who repents, than over all the righteous who have no need to repent. Again, Jesus' audience must have been silently seething. The Parable of the Prodigal Son is the coup de grâce, a story of a son who broke all the rules and yet was taken back by his father.

The Father searches for us all and rejoices with "all of heaven" to find his lost son or daughter (Luke 15:7, 10, 32).

In the previous parables, both the shepherd who finds his sheep and the woman who discovers her coin call their friends and neighbors and say to them, "Rejoice with me." Yet the rejoicing is, by comparison, subdued. The sheep and the coin are passive: they "are found." Here there is greater emphasis on choice. The one who was lost has a free, inner conversion, a "coming to himself," that enables him to actively return to God and to family. Such joy cannot be contained, but has the power to overwhelm God's entire household.

JUSTICE IN THE FATHER'S HOUSE

Each of us starts out like the prodigal son, far away from the Father's house. This is our real, theological situation. St. Paul describes it starkly: "There is no one who is righteous, not even one....All have sinned and fall short of the glory of God" (Rom 3:10, 23). However, in Christ we have peace with God, access to the Father, and the right to inherit all that belongs to the one Son. We are no longer lost, no longer slaves, but God's own beloved children. Yet many Christians identify with the older son, the faithful son.

Why did Jesus include the elder son in this parable? The elder son prefers the system of "earning" things for himself through years of service. He never questions his father. He feels that what he receives from his father is out of strict justice. The obedient son felt comfortable within the predictable world of the rules that governed his life. How unfair then, when his brother and his father break all the rules he had been so carefully keeping! His father's love and generosity are like a slap in his face.

The father, however, responds with the answer of one who seeks to empower: "Son, you are always with me, and all that is mine is yours, but we had to celebrate and rejoice, because this brother of yours was dead and has come to life; he was lost and has been found" (Luke 15:31–32). With these words, this father uses his authority to empower his child—to mercy. He challenges this son to maturity, to see himself as an equal to his father and part of the family. It is a hard lesson. The older son is still too taken aback to respond in a positive manner. His father's sense of justice is shocking, for he rejoices over a son who should enrage him. Nevertheless, the father now challenges the older boy to a conversion of his own, saying that "we" have to do this thing, for it is right for us both. Just as the father left the younger son open to make his own choice, he does the same for the older. He does not order the older son to obey, but invites him, as an equal, to be as merciful and gracious as his father is, even though it is difficult. This is the astounding way God practices authority with his beloved children.

If family life is indeed evolving, and if rules in family relationships are being defined by the individuals involved, this parable presents mercy and empowerment as the direction we should be evolving toward. These values should be fostered in Christian family life, especially as ideals for fathers. This is important for women as well. For women have come to share in some of the negative aspects of power dynamics that have been attributed to men because of our workaholic, consumerist culture. The ideal of mutuality presents a way of keeping in check the extremes of these forms of competition, manipulation, and exploitation, no matter who is being adversely affected.

CONCLUSION

Family life benefits from the greater partnership between men and women expressed here as mutuality. Just as women have enriched the professions in their own ways, men enrich the family with their presence and care, and are enriched in turn by their children. Everyone is gifted by this mutuality in family life. The presence of the father and his love in the family is a far more apt metaphor for God the Father than the distant, unapproachable patriarch that often presided over families of yesteryear.

As women and mothers, we want partnership in raising children and partnership in life. It is not "women's work" to raise children, but "parent's work." The quality, not so much the

quantity, of time we give to our children can lay the foundation
for their health and happiness as adults. All of this points to an
ancient truth, one which we have difficulty putting into action
today, that raising children is not meant to be the work of a solitary individual or even a solitary couple, but of a community.
This community begins with a mother and child, welcomes the
father, and is integrated into the large society. Each family stands
in need of the love and support of a nurturing community in
order to thrive. Community comes to the assistance of single
parents and families in crisis. It shares in the joys as well as the
struggles. It is to community that we turn in the next chapter.

ENCOUNTER AND PRACTICE

Encounter

Close the door to your office or room, or retreat to a
secluded spot outside. Focus yourself by lighting a candle, by
dwelling on the beauty of nature like water in a garden fountain
or flowers, or by simply spending a few minutes with your eyes
closed. You may also create a space for prayer by placing an icon
or holy image in a corner of your room. Before you begin, try to
imagine how God is looking at you, just as you are in this
moment. Offer God a sign of reverence (bow, kneel, or just pay
attention to your breath).

First, ask God for the gift of knowing him as your Father.
In the spirit of Jesus' description, imagine "how much more" the
heavenly Father desires to give you if you only ask. What is the
"much more" for you?

Next, ask for the Spirit to assist you to call out, "Abba,
Father" (Rom 8:15), to empower you and give you fullness of
mercy so you can turn back to the Father's house and find joy.
(You may do this exercise using the text of the parable of the
shepherd with the lost sheep or the woman who sweeps the
house to find her coin, also in Luke 15). End with a thanksgiving
prayer for the banquet that is about to begin. Ask yourself,
"What image of God do I have? Do I hold onto an image of God

that is exacting and condemning? Can I begin to see God empowering me? Giving me good things? Showing me mercy, even when I hurt others as the prodigal son did? How can I communicate a renewed attitude to my children and spouse?

Practice

1. *Mutuality*. Identify one job that your spouse is usually responsible for. Ask him or her permission to take this job for one week. The stipulation is that he or she is not allowed to critique how the task is done. (You may also do this exercise by trading tasks for a week.) After the week is up, answer the following questions in writing:
   - Did I enjoy or dislike this task?
   - Do I have a better appreciation for the contribution made to the family through doing this task? Have I taken this service for granted in the past?
   - Is there one task I don't want to do? Can I do it anyway, out of a spirit of service? (Toilets are a good place to start. Mother Teresa of Calcutta made a practice of cleaning the toilet whenever she visited one of her sister communities.) Take ten minutes to share your feelings about this experience with your spouse and express gratitude.

2. *Fathering*. Put away whatever could distract you, like a newspaper or computer. Ask your child to sit down with you. A snack works well to draw children to the table for conversation at any age. If your child is younger, ask him or her questions; for older ones, try letting your child ask the questions. Here are some examples:
   - Did you have any dreams last night? (Once my five-year-old told me a wonderful dream about being in the ocean swimming with sea creatures. He was swimming with a shark which suddenly turned into his stuffed animal, Otter Pup, and then his foot touched a deadly jelly, which also transformed into

another animal toy, the white fox, Dox. It was nice
to hear this, since we had been praying for an end to
bad dreams. Maybe God was answering his
prayers?)

- Who is your favorite person at school?
- What would be your ideal fun day or night out?

This practice will not work if it's done once a
year. When we ask our children questions regularly (or let children question us), we bring our
children out, show we are interested in them and
in their perspective. This is a key aspect in any
relationship-building. It allows us to get a picture
of what is going on in them, both the inner and
the outer child.

After you have this conversation, ask yourself: What did I learn? What did I impart? Did I
enjoy this? How did it compare to the last time
we talked? Take a few notes in a journal so you
don't forget the amazing things your children
say to you. Try to imagine these times with your
child as a solid foundation for a later, adult relationship with him or her. Talking with your children will do more for them in the long term than
lots of extracurricular activities and will equip
them for all life's many relationships.

CHAPTER SIX

Blessed Are You

The Future of Motherhood

And all in the crowd were trying to touch him, for power
came out from him and healed all of them.

Luke 7:19

This verse describes Jesus moments before he gave the world
Christianity's great charter, the Beatitudes. A great many disciples were present and people from miles around who wanted to
be healed and to hear him speak. As they listened in that strange
silence that sometimes falls upon a large gathering, Jesus gave a
startling blessing:

> "Blessed are you who are poor,
>   for yours is the kingdom of God.
> "Blessed are you who are hungry now,
>   for you will be filled.
> "Blessed are you who weep now,
>   for you will laugh.
> "Blessed are you when people hate you, and when they
>   exclude you, revile you, and defame you on account of
>   the Son of Man. Rejoice in that day and leap for joy,
>   for surely your reward is great in heaven; for that is
>   what their ancestors did to the prophets."

Jesus then curses those who feel full and satisfied; the list of
woes mirrors the list of blessings he has just given. He closes

with the central Christian challenge: "Love your enemies, do good to those who hate you, bless those who curse you, pray for those who abuse you" (Luke 6:17–28).

The Beatitudes, also called the Sermon on the Mount, and their companion teachings might seem to glorify suffering. As mothers, nothing irks us more than the suggestion, let alone an injunction, that we meekly embrace poverty or misfortune. We pursue the opposite. For the sake of our children, we are dedicated to creating the best possible future for their well-being, health, and prosperity. We want them to be taken care of and to prosper, not to suffer poverty, hunger, or sorrow. Furthermore, if we ourselves are poor, hungry, and sorrowing, won't that hinder us from taking care of them? It is not easy for us to accept the Beatitudes. So we may be tempted to romanticize them instead, or leave them to someone else, the professional religious—nuns, priests, pastors, and missionaries.

Neither option, however, is desirable if we are seeking holiness. As is always true with Scripture, we must ponder its meaning to find its truth for us in our particular circumstances. The Greek word used in the Beatitudes for *blessed* is *makarios*, from the root *mak*, or "large and lengthy." It is the root of our prefix *macro* that means something done on a large scale. It also signifies "the nature of that which is the highest good."[1] Details from the gospel help us to better understand "blessing."

Jesus is doing two things in this passage. First, he is teaching. The multitude is so large that he has to go up on a hill to avoid being crushed by those flocking to hear his words. Second, Jesus is healing. He is in full form today, power "goes out" from him just by a mere touch. Like the woman with the hemorrhage who reached out to grab the hem of his clothing and was healed, everyone in the crowd tried to touch Jesus; here too the power came out from him and healed those who touched him with faith; the gospel says "all of them."

Notice that Jesus is addressing two different audiences: the crowd of disciples and the multitude. In Luke's Gospel, Jesus turns away from the multitude (those he was healing and consoling) toward his disciples (those he was teaching) and says to the disciples, "Blessed are you..."

Luke was a physician. He must have witnessed some dire cases and must have been deeply moved by the misery of humanity. He was not going to pretend there was anything "blessed" about suffering. When Luke presents Jesus to us, in the middle of a multitude of sick people, Jesus is comforting these people. He is not prolonging their suffering, or in any way lauding it. He is ending it. However, then Jesus turns away from the people down on the plains and toward his disciples: "He looked up at his disciples" and spoke. In this "looking up," there is a shift in action from healing to teaching. Jesus turns to his disciples, his students, to say, "Do you see all this illness and need, this poverty and suffering? As my followers, you will not be seated upon thrones apart from the suffering of humanity. You will be in it with them. You will share it and carry it, heal and embrace them right along with me. But because you are with me, and because you embrace all humanity in my name, all that before could only ever be a curse, will be a blessing. You will bless and heal alongside me. You will possess the kingdom of heaven, you will be filled, you will laugh and leap into the air for sheer joy."

The Beatitudes show us the work of Jesus is to heal and mitigate suffering in the world—the healing part. But they take us further, because they assert that, for his disciples, Jesus is also transforming the very meaning of suffering—this is Jesus' teaching. Christ offers us the highest good, the blessing par excellence, by promising that by following him we ultimately are victorious over the key evils of this life: poverty, hunger, sorrow, and hatred. And he offers the fourfold weapon of victory: love, do good, bless, and pray in the face of that evil. He challenges us, that is, to compassion.

The Beatitudes usher in a new kind of blessedness. They signify that God's blessing is not limited to material success, wealth, status, or even health, for that matter. God blesses humankind right in the midst of all the many aspects of our humanity, including adversity. Like the Buddhist value of compassion, the Beatitudes plunge us into the world as it is and invite us to share, to be in com-passion, with others. Rather than glorify suffering, the Beatitudes promise the only way to be victorious over each and every instance of human suffering. God

honors this compassion and sees a sacred kinship with his own
divine compassion. Again, the Buddhist insight is that greeting
another person with the word *namaste* means that "the divine in
me greets the divine in you." *Bless* in Hebrew means "to bow
the knee," as if God were greeting the divine in us at this very
moment when we show compassion.[2]

A BLESSING FOR MOTHERS

There is a long history of blessing in Jewish faith and culture. In Genesis God blessed each part of creation. He gave a
special blessing to the first parents, making them in the divine
image. God blessed them and said, be fruitful and multiply,
showing the largess of his love. God blessed the day of rest.
Blessing also appears in the psalms: children are a blessing (Ps
127:5) and those who fear the Lord are blessed (Ps 128:1).

When Mary heard the angel bless her as "favored" by
God, God was inviting her to become mother of the promised
Messiah. We may assume she knew Scripture well because she
was "troubled" and wondered what such a momentous greeting might mean. Mary also heard words of blessing as she
entered the house of Elizabeth: "Blessed are you for your firm
believing, that the words spoken to you would come to pass."
She responds: "My soul proclaims the greatness of the Lord and
my spirit finds joy in God, my Savior. He who is mighty has
done great things for me." God blesses her because of her "firm
believing," and it is nothing less than the action of God to save
his people. Recognizing this, Mary praises God. There is a
back-and-forth, a dialogue, of blessing that leads her to gratitude and joy.

If a woman has never before experienced the Beatitudes,
motherhood is her opportunity. Their poverty and humility is
contained in motherhood. During pregnancy, something within
becomes knit together with the basic neediness of humanity. We
learn the meaning of complete dependence. We go through the
drama of giving birth, where the unexpected always seems to
crop up. Our bodies take us through the pedagogy of the hum-

ble beginning that is a fact of every human life. We taste innocence, the complete absence of evil in a child, reminding us that
human beings are originally good and unspoiled. Giving birth
makes us know things in our bodies we may not have consciously considered before. It wakes us up to compassion, as we
see the fragility of life and the shocking truth of a unique being.
Motherhood opens us up to poverty and riches, sorrow, and also
joy—the paradox of Jesus' Beatitudes.

Read the Beatitudes, then put them aside and see how you
feel. Let them be the starting point for your own dialogue with
God, the back-and-forth of family life.

Motherhood is a taste of the largesse of God, the amazing
goodness of creation that keeps on going each and every day.
There is something stunning about a baby. When they are
young, we are still mystified by our children, but as they grow
we must be reminded over the years. We get glimpses of it in the
things they say or how they look at us. Pictures they draw and
poems they write betray this original goodness. Sometimes we
forget. Cynicism and stereotypes and inattention get in the way.
Yet that early nesting instinct, the one that kicks in even before
the child is born, reminds us to return to the sacred, the place of
quiet where we can enjoy for a few minutes the macro, the great
goodness, of each child, the blessing. The kingdom of God is in
these relationships that transcend materiality. Children are often
the ones who remind us of this.

One Easter I gave my five-year-old slips of paper in his
Easter basket, with the words *Golden Hour* printed on them, for
him to cash in when he wanted to spend time with me. When my
children were old enough to write, they started giving me little
pieces of paper too. These little tickets woke me up to the real-
ization that they valued a little time with me more than many
other things.

Parents know what a golden hour is. It's a taste of the
blessedness proclaimed in the Beatitudes, as we put aside our
"important affairs" to play with a child. Jesus did this when he
welcomed the children despite the protests of his disciples. A
golden hour with our children can make us happily poor; it can
make us weep at our child's hidden innocence; it can make us

hungry for a different kind of life, a slower pace; it can make us hate the things that get in the way.

A golden hour might help us to see our children as the path to God and not a distraction from God. Keeping the Beatitudes alive in family life is countercultural. Families are threatened by attitudes that harden us and distract us from the personal and intimate sphere of relationship-building within the family and with our neighbors near and far. We are like Martha, who begged Jesus to tell Mary to give up sitting at his feet to listen to him in order to help with the work of hospitality. But Jesus told her that she was worried over too many things, but the one thing necessary was what Mary had chosen—"the better part." "The better part" for parents is the same; it is to spend time with our children, not just any time, but the kind that builds relationship with them. This is what Mary chose as she sat with Jesus, even though there was work to be done. It's easy to miss the blessing. Let us look for a moment at some things that get in the way.

STEREOTYPES OF MOTHERS— ALIENATION OF WOMEN

Stereotypes can cause us to either romanticize motherhood or become cynical about it. They can become obstacles to following Christ as teachers and healers who live the Beatitudes.

A stereotype is an assumption about a whole group (their race, religion, or vocation) that judges that group in a negative or positive way. The word comes from the Greek *stere*, which means "solid." In sociology, a stereotype means "a standard conception or image invested with special meaning and held in common by members of a group."[3] It also has the connotation of lacking originality or inventiveness. A stereotype can take away the creative edge with which we look at our own vocation and can paralyze our thinking.

Mothers have been stereotyped in "positive" ways: the "good mother," who has no faults and no needs of her own; the "home-beautiful mother," whose house is perpetually clean and whose laundry is always done; the "meek mother," who never yells at her kids and never, ever gets angry; the "career-track maven," who does it all and succeeds at all she does; the "angel mother," who is devoted to God and volunteers all the time, while never neglecting her children, her home, or her own needs, which anyway are few.

There are also negative stereotypes: "helicopter moms"; "mother bears"; the "perfect-child moms," whose children can do no wrong; "PTA moms," who turn ugly when they turn political; "drug moms," who are hopelessly addicted and want to stay that way; "welfare mothers," who enjoy being on welfare; "irresponsible-driver moms," who are not careful with car seat laws; "crazy celebrity moms."

Stereotypes objectify people. They foster criticism and kill constructive critique and intelligent debate. Worst, they cloud our minds so we subconsciously feel driven to avoid being like the stereotypes we hate most, meanwhile missing the simple fact of our own blessed lives. The negative energy that stereotypes produce can also incite women to attack each other for the choices they have made. Some engage in "mommy wars," setting up opposing camps, creating a state of a perpetual energy drain. They blog at each other and vent. These so-called wars, however, take us away from the work we could be doing, constructive work for ourselves and our families.

Stereotypes perpetuate alienation and division. A person makes a small observation that often contains a kernel of truth. Then a generalization is made, and the particular example extends to an entire group like cancer grows on a healthy cell. When we can generalize about a group, it is easy to objectify, criticize, and judge. Fostering judgmental attitudes can even cause people to feel better about themselves. A more insidious side effect, however, is the way stereotypes perpetuate blindness, ignorance of the need for constructive self-criticism and a healthy reform of our own lives. As long as we are busy pointing the finger at others, we won't have the energy and focus necessary to examine ourselves.

Mothers share many of the same concerns and are blessed with complementary insights and wisdom. This is grounds for women coming closer together, not being alienated from each

other. Furthermore, when women criticize each other for different ways of mothering, it is often one stereotype that is pit
against another. Yet neither stereotype exists in the real world in
any meaningful way. Human nature (not just the media) focuses
on the negative and sensational, on what divides instead of what
unites. So mommy wars abound that are largely a waste of time.
These cultural squabbles keep women from becoming a greater
force for positive change for themselves and their children.

Jesus has advice for his disciple-mothers. As he told the disciples on the hillside the day of the Sermon on the Mount, he
tells us to be with our sisters, to accompany those who need
healing, and to mitigate the suffering of others. We do this for
our children first, on a daily basis, but we also do it for the children of others and, hopefully, for each other. Sociologists identify the family as the foundational building block of society. One
could say it is essentially communal. Bringing up children
requires the collaborative effort of many, and so healthy mothering cannot be an individualistic experience. It is precisely by
sharing each other's experiences, and our responses to them, that
we can grow as women and individuals through motherhood.
The challenge, however, is to acknowledge each other's experience and to listen and be respectful even if we cannot agree on
particular issues. We can be a society or a rabble.

Some issues—such as abortion or the debate over same-sex
marriage—divide women just as they do the general population.
But others—like the need for every child to receive adequate
health care and a good education—are clearly works of mercy
that can unite us. We can find much common ground where we
stand right now; that is, in the concrete, daily concerns we
encounter in family life. Even issues that ostensibly divide us can
be points of unity. What if Christian mothers who self-identify
as "pro-life" worked with women who self-identify as "pro-
choice" to offer education and care for girls who choose to keep
a child? This too is a choice. The exercise of working together
can change the nature of the debate and show a path forward in
the spirit of healing. Mitigation of suffering, as Jesus showed us
in the Beatitudes, is our first priority.

As Christian mothers and disciples, we must find ways to let our voices be heard that do not involve attacks and condemnation. It is our responsibility as followers of Christ to seek common ground on issues and to work together to ease suffering. We have the greater share of the burden to build bridges and seek peace. The longer set of Beatitudes in Matthew includes these three additional blessings: "Blessed are the merciful, for they will receive mercy. Blessed are the pure of heart, for they will see God. Blessed are the peacemakers, for they will be called children of God" (Matt 5:7–9).

NEW MODELS FOR THE FUTURE

Mothers and others who care for children form the people of tomorrow. The people of tomorrow will determine whether we live in war or peace, whether we use up the world's water and energy or find ways to conserve them responsibly, whether we allow people to die of hunger and disease or find ways to feed the world and tend to the sick.

Much in the world around us is antithetical to the core of the gospel: love, do good works, bless and pray for one's enemies, for those who hate you, for those who curse you, and for those who abuse you (Luke 7). In view of the gospel, it really does make a difference whether we teach the people of tomorrow the foundational lesson that they are loved unconditionally. This is not so that our children can feel good about themselves. It is so they can feel and act out of a sense of their own value, in order to take responsibility for their lives and the world around them. No one can give what he or she doesn't possess. Each generation needs the tools to care for those around them and not to simply consume. These are the challenges that are met everyday by mothers and fathers and other dedicated souls, and it bears repeating: how we bring up our children has repercussions for the future of our planet.

Imagine God blessing mothers. Imagine the one who set the cosmos in motion and who is Mother to All Life saying, "This is your time to lead."

Passing on the Blessing

Parents teach constantly. We teach with our words, our attitudes, and, most of all, our schedules—what we model in our behavior. Some lessons are practical, like eating regularly and socializing so we can function at school and work. But we also pass on less-tangible things. We communicate invisible messages about our philosophy of life, such as whether we think the world is mostly a safe place or a dangerous place, whether people are fundamentally good or evil, whether hard work pays off, whether certain kinds of work are better left for others to do. We also invisibly communicate how to treat others.

Too often parents ignore the influence they have to form their children. Some have said that one of the best things parents can do for their children is to work on the state of their own physical and spiritual health. Responding to our own call to holiness will have an affect on our children, far more than what we say about God or faith. This is the fundamental legacy we give them. Even then, they must ultimately choose either to accept this legacy freely or to decline faith. We can only offer to share our faith experience. The risk of our children's freedom can be terrifying to parents who want them to believe and find God's blessing. Yet our culture makes us want to minimize risk in every area of our lives.

As our children grow up and start to move away from us, parents naturally want to protect them from harm. Yet sometimes we translate this to mean protecting them from conflict, pain, or discomfort of any kind. Part of the logic of the current obsession with comparative shopping—for everything from the best schools to the best clothing or music lessons—has its tentacles in this fear of failure. We think it is best if we prepare our children for the world by padding their "resumes" with extracurricular activities, beginning by enrolling them in only the best preschool. These things are all good as far as they go. But no activity or training, no matter how amazing, has the capacity to prepare a child for the challenges of life. Unconditional love from their parents will. How do we communicate such love? If love remains the most important thing we can offer our children, why does it seem so elusive?

In their book *The Blessing*, John Trent and Gary Smalley give simple practices of blessing based on practices in the Old Testament. They describe a fivefold blessing to help make unconditional love a reality in daily life: meaningful touch, a spoken message, attaching high value to the one being blessed, picturing a special future for the one being blessed, and active commitment to fulfill the blessing.[4] The authors devised these steps of blessing in response to the pain in the families they counseled. They discovered, through their work with families, the pain suffered by those who have missed out on this blessing. According to them, being intentional about blessing our children can help them far into the future. As we look at each of these blessings, they apply not only to our children but also to us. We will likely find areas in our own lives where we lack a sense that we are loved. Don't we often imagine that God receives us only after we have dressed up, confessed our sins, or in some other way made ourselves "acceptable"?

The psychologist David Benner writes about a childhood need to "secure love by presenting ourselves in the most favorable light." So it is not only that we are trying to show our children that we love them, but we ourselves are challenged to accept, at the core of our being, God's unconditional love—*now*, before we "pretty up," before we even get around to confession. As St. John famously said, "In this is love, not that we loved God but that he loved us" (1 John 4:10). When we accept and give a blessing, we can gradually outgrow the need to slavishly present ourselves in "the most favorable light." Accepting love equips us to give love. As Benner also notes, when we grow in comprehending that God loves and accepts "the actual self, the real me," it frees us to love others in this way.[5]

That Hebrew meaning of *bless*, "to bend the knee," comes into play here. When we accept a child as he or she is, we help that child come into contact with his or her true self. We make them comfortable in their own skin. And we show them that they are sacred—each one—to us and even to God. This prepares them for the real world: when they can lovingly accept the real self.

Fivefold Blessing

The first blessing that Trent and Smalley describe is physical touch. They tell the story of a little girl frightened by a thunderstorm. When the storm is at its height and she can no longer stand to be alone in her bed, she tears off to her parents' room, hops on the bed, and shouts, "Daddy, hug me, hug me!" Her father responds, "Don't worry, honey. The Lord will protect you." She says, "I know that, Daddy, but right now I need someone with skin on!"[6]

People need touch. Meaningful touch is a direct, physical blessing that sends a message of love, one our children need throughout their lives, no matter how big they get. Studies have been done to show that babies cannot develop if they are not held and touched.

As our children grow older, we tend to stop hugging, kissing, and holding hands with them. We get busy and we assume they no longer want or need this. Yet they do. Holding and hugging, a reassuring hand on the head, maybe even tickling or wrestling and other forms of play can serve this purpose. Touch allows us to love without words. It also helps us mend the broken moments that accompany daily living. It reminds us that we can trust the basic given that we are wanted, held, accepted, and loved. Jesus was constantly touching the people who came to him for healing. He blessed the children, resting his hands on them and letting them come close. This is the first and most basic aspect of blessing given by the authors, and I would include the healing element, like a daily restorative.[7]

The second blessing is the spoken word. We should not assume our children already know we love them. They don't. "A blessing becomes so only when it is spoken."[8] Many things can get in the way of spoken blessings, such as hyperactivity, embarrassment, or simply the belief that words are superfluous. We put off saying, "I love you," because we think it must be so obvious. Trent and Smalley argue that silence can spell indifference to children, when they never hear words of blessing that spell love and acceptance. Why would a child have to be constantly reassured? It is not only children. We too have to be reassured in our adult relationships. Who has not heard of the romantic desire to hear words of love from the beloved, or the desire of a wife or husband to hear the words *I love you?* It is part of our human makeup to need this reassurance. The home is the place where it is safe to speak in this way. Words of love, praise, or gratitude are often quite personal communications, not something to be said in front of the Girl Scout troop or the best friend who is there on a sleepover. This intimacy is part of the sacred, to be respected.

When we give a spoken blessing, it can also have a transforming effect on us. It helps make us honest about our own feelings and it models for our children how to be open about theirs.[9] The longer we go without uttering words of blessing, the harder it is to say them. It may even feel foreign or insincere when we do. If we begin when our children are young, and continue as they grow older, it won't be so awkward. We can use various ways of communicating a blessing to a child of any age; for example, words of appreciation and thanks also communicate acceptance and love.[10]

The third kind of blessing is attaching high value to the one being blessed. It calls attention to the particular gift and beauty of each child. The authors refer to examples of blessing in Scripture to illustrate how a word picture can honor a child. Isaac blessed Jacob saying, "Surely the smell of my son is like the smell of a field which the LORD has blessed" (Gen 27:27). Isaac has his own way of thinking about Jacob, a sensation that conjures up Jacob's preciousness. Whenever Isaac smells a field, he thinks of the very fragrance of blessing on Jacob! In sharing this, Isaac shows Jacob his love and appreciation. Word pictures can concretize any trait or event in a child's life that illustrates something that makes him or her dear to others.

Fourth, picturing a special future helps a child to believe in his or her potential to do good in the world. Hope, optimism, realism, and a positive attitude are the fruits of this kind of blessing. As stewards of our children's abilities, we can help our children picture success based on their actual talents, help shed light on their pathway, and help them find their genuine purpose. This does not send the message: you can do anything you want if you put your mind to it (no one can do "anything"). Instead, the message is more concrete. It gives the "hope and direction that is part of picturing meaningful goals" that suit the individual.[11] Notice that this approach is also cautionary, for it does not project onto our children what *we* would have wanted to do or become. Instead, when we value our children's future, we encourage them to be excited about their actual potential to work hard to achieve what they desire. In this blessing, we also share the truth that the Lord himself gives our child a future with hope— that he himself truly knows and encourages each child in the direction they should go. For what will it profit our child to gain the whole world but lose himself in the process?

To bless our children requires action, not just talk. The fifth blessing is commitment. The authors tell us to pray for our children, commit ourselves to their best interests, and discipline them.[12] Communicating, sharing activities, listening to our children with full attention are challenging enterprises. The blessing can be given as part of the routine of life: riding a bike to school, making dinner together, or playing a favorite game. Yet offering a blessing through these simple activities requires a commitment to imbue them with the meaningful touch, the spoken words, the valuing, and the hope that were just described. These are truly exercises that bring joy and are worth every minute of our effort. Making blessing a part of daily life is one way we live the Beatitudes.

MOTHER-DISCIPLES: SAINTS, HEROES AND MODELS OF HOPE

Motherhood is trivialized and the work of real women is ignored when stereotypes prevail. The media use stereotypes to sensationalize and sell stories, advertisers use them to sell products, and politicians use them to manipulate and secure votes. This draws people away from meaningful communication and collaboration. It erodes respect because it is easier to mock a type or a concept than a real person. It is the real people, the women who work to be a blessing and provide a future for their families, who can inspire us:

- Women who open their door to strangers, friends, and family alike
- Women who struggle to survive in the face of violence and war
- Women who live with the reality of a chronically ill child
- Women who struggle with a husband's infidelity, who offer loving forgiveness, but who refuse to enable sexual addiction
- Women who dedicate themselves to the search for God in the midst of everything
- Women who practice the virtue of friendship
- Women who bake
- Women who tackle the work of daily life with humor and joy
- Women who use their talents in their work or career to enrich others
- Women who are patient and kind out of strength, and who put their anger at the service of justice

When I think of women I would consider "saints," it is those whom I see turning their hearts and minds toward others in love, even in the midst of their own share of life's difficulties and sorrows. These women may not be Christian or even religious. Yet their lives proclaim who they are, raising my consciousness of the gift and strength we have at our disposal as mothers.

Consciousness-raising is another way to speak of becoming aware. Awareness is our capacity to see what is. Human beings are limited in what we can perceive at any given time about ourselves and about the world around us. Awareness is not a state of nirvana in which we can know everything, something for a select few to strive after. A more accurate picture of awareness is that of a growing plant, steadily and gradually pushing its roots deeper down and expanding its branches further up. It is this expansive and progressive quality of awareness that allows us to gradually know what life is, what it *means*, and what impact we can have on the world. Growing awareness is as essential to human growth as the sun is to the plant.

For the man or woman who is growing in this way, becoming a parent is an opportunity for spiritual awakening. The practice of growing awareness is the antithesis of stereotyping. It enables us to know and open our mind's eye to the complexity of life, but also the simplicity of our human reality: life is a gift that is a good in itself.

Celebrating the lives of the women we admire and who encourage us creates a solidarity with them that gives us the strength to follow our own calling. The saints, whether living or dead, whether canonized publicly or honored privately (as a beloved parent might be), are friends and mentors who help us to live well. They encourage us not to simply imitate them, but to emulate them by walking down our own path more faithfully. Some saints who had mystical experiences or great suffering may seem unreal or extreme. Yet we are called to love the same God, to walk our own path with their intensity of love, to be conscious of our call to intimacy with God himself. In the next chapter, we will look at how living the blessing at home can help our families become a blessing for the world.

ENCOUNTER AND PRACTICE

Encounter

Find a place of solitude where you are comfortable and no one will interrupt you. As in former exercises, you may be outside on a secluded park bench, in your room, your office, or a place you have prepared specifically for prayer. Begin by paying attention to your breath. Breath is a constant in your life, so listen to it, feel the sensations of breath fill and empty your lungs. Let it calm your mind.

- See how God is looking at you. How do you imagine God? As a father, a mother, a friend who values you?
- Ask God for the grace of blessing—to know how you've been blessed in the past and to receive a new blessing from God today.

- Go back in your memory to an event in your life that was a blessing. Recall how old you were, what you looked like. Recall or imagine the other people who were there with you. Remember what you did and said and what the people with you did and said. What was the experience like? What did you see, feel, hear, touch, or taste? Why was this a blessing for you?
- Give thanks for this one event. Share your impressions of this with the Lord, as well as anything else that comes to mind. Ask God to help you see how you have been blessed by him and how your future is also blessed.

Practice

1. *Word Pictures*. Make a word picture for each of your children. You may need to recall something particular about his or her life to get started. For example, my son, Joseph, was born in North Carolina in April, as we were enjoying a beautiful spring. But the morning he was born, the air took on a crisp, cold quality. The trees held their breath and suddenly it began to snow! Newspapers featured pictures of amazed faces looking up at the falling snow. When I saw the snow outside my hospital window, it made me feel like heaven was just delighted about Joseph's birth. And I was so delighted to become a mother that day. This story symbolizes how Joseph is dear to me, like Isaac was reminded of Jacob whenever he smelled the fragrant field; I am reminded of Joseph when I see delicate flakes of snow falling. The picture helps me envision the gift of this individual. Joseph's name means "the Lord adds," sometimes interpreted as "prosperity," and snow reminds me of this abundance of grace.

   A special memory like this can serve as a word picture. It's like a secret code that only the listeners and speaker comprehend. It can provide a perpetual security blanket for your child, one you never have to take away, one he or she is meant to keep. It highlights a particular person and the delight he or she gives you that nobody else can.

2. *Family Blessing in the Home* (based on a Jewish blessing ritual). Prepare a special food or dessert your family likes. Set a table with lit candles. Lay your hands on the head of each child (both father and mother should do this, one at a time). Using any special names you have for each (nickname, word picture, or a verse from Scripture), pray over each and ask God to bless their future. This is a "vehicle for communicating a sense of identity, love, meaning, and acceptance."[13]

3. *New Rituals.* Discover your own practices of blessing to suit your family and situation. You may start by telling stories during or after meals, or any time you are together. Stories about each child can quickly give a sense of how they are valued in a light-hearted and accepting way. This can heal a child of the hurts of daily life and help him or her understand that their worth doesn't depend on performance or success. For a few minutes, you are focused on one child, and in a world where our attention is continuously snatched away from our children, this, by itself, is a blessing to them.

CHAPTER SEVEN

Come Inherit the Kingdom

Justice, One Child at a Time

> We fail to recognize the family as the heart and soul of doing justice. It is the place where justice is first learned and practiced, and the place where we begin to turn the world upside down.[1]
>
> Bonnie J. Miller-McLemore

CHILDREN OF GOD'S REIGN: A PERSONAL STORY

The children ran after me along the mountain ridge, where their makeshift huts huddled against the sky. They clamored for more of the candy I had been handing out. The rugged, volcano-dotted landscape of Guatemala, with blue Lake Atitlán shining in the distance, gave the impression of an earthly paradise. Yet this was no paradise. These children and their parents had fled their homes on the plantation in protest against oppressive landowners. They were destitute.

The children laughed and gathered around me as I turned to face them. "Lo siento mucho," I said. "I'm sorry, but I'm out of candy!" A second later, I remembered a small flask of blessed oil I carried in my pocket. "Who wants a blessing with this holy oil?" I asked, hopefully. To my utter amazement, the children exploded with joyous excitement. "I do! I do!" One little boy pointed to a younger boy who could only have been his younger brother. "Give him a blessing first. He really needs one. He's been very, very naughty."

So I blessed them, wondering secretly what they saw in this oil, made from olives I had helped pick at a retreat house in Northern California, and which was used there for healing services. What strength or consolation did they find here, what *dulce* ("sweet") for the spirit?

My travel companions were already down the hill and calling to me. As I said my goodbyes, I turned to our Guatemalan guide, and he smiled at me. Then he uttered words I will never forget: "You are one of us!"

Why would he say those words? I was a Westerner and lived far away. I have never had to worry about violence at my door, or starvation, or abuse, like these war-torn survivors. How did a little blessed oil overrule the differences between us and unify us despite so many divides of culture and history?

That day the children became my teachers and the poor showed me a different kind of wealth. They showed me how joy can rush through the heart through the simplest of means. It was as if God had pulled back a corner of the covering that blocked my routine view of life, to the hidden reality underneath, the lasting reign of God.

APOCALYPSE: TURNING BACK THE COVERS

This story is a personal "life parable." Each of us has such stories, which summon us to pay attention and ponder. Such experiences can be hard to articulate at first, but over time, as we treasure the memory in our heart, they may become clearer. Sometimes our life parables change and grow over the years.

Instead of fading with time, a particular memory can offer new insights.

In this spirit of ongoing discovery, Mary pondered the things that happened to her, as we read in the Gospel of Luke. Pondering can strike us deeply and show us something beyond what we normally perceive with our senses, the "already, but not yet" of the fulfillment of God's promises. The word *apocalypse*, of Greek origin, expresses this glimpse, this foretaste of God's reign. It means to draw back a covering so that what is hidden can suddenly be seen: the truth of things beyond their immediate appearance.

The life parable above is one that consistently calls me to ponder the mystery of the reign of God. Like a "small gospel" that can inspire and challenge me, it comes alive each time I revisit it. It holds at least three hidden graces for me that inspire me in new ways now that I am a mother.

1. Running Out of Candy: Destitute Before God

A mother is constantly feeding others. There is no question of substituting something else for daily bread. For mothers, running out is not an option; and bread is just the beginning. Running out is something every mother fears for her children: a lack of nutritious food, clean water, a home, health care, and education—the basics.

The children on that ridge in Guatemala are a reminder of the precariousness of life, its fragility, and the dangers of running low on whatever it is our child may need at a given time. We find out what this fragility feels like when our own child is injured or becomes ill. When we tremble with worry and pray with all our strength for our child to recover, we know in the most concrete way possible how fragile life really is. Perhaps for this reason, the hardships of other families near and far can strike women and mothers with such intensity. Our own children and the depths of love we feel for them make it all too clear what is at stake. We may become overwhelmed by a gut reaction to the plight of others and more aware of all kinds of people who, like children, are small and vulnerable, powerless or afraid.

A mother's deepest desire for each child is to see him or her thrive. This desire comes alive in us in pregnancy and is accompanied by protective instincts that prepare us to defend our child from danger. Mothers have been likened to bears or warriors because of this instinct for our children's well-being. As each child grows, we naturally desire to foster each one's particular talents and gifts, to help each become the beautiful and successful human being that he or she alone can be. When all is well and our children are thriving, we witness the power of youth, the brilliant thrust of energy and success in our child's young life. As we foster this growth, the life, goodness, health, and blessing for our families are their own rewards.

Sometimes, however, we can be trapped when our desire to provide the best for our children is too narrowly defined in terms of economic success. For example, Aunt Sadie is sure her nephew is going to become a prominent surgeon, meaning that he is going to make a lot of money as a prominent surgeon. Parents can subconsciously drive their children to fulfill dreams that have nothing to do with their true, individually given gifts and potential. When this happens, a rebellious child may flee his or her responsibilities to reject living out the plans others have made about his or her future. A dutiful child might waste a great deal of time working in an area that does not satisfy the heart or call forth his or her talents.

Parents usually know instinctively that money cannot be the most important aspect of their children's future. Once fundamental needs are met, there are other, less tangible needs. Children will need to develop a sense of meaning, fulfillment, and purpose in their own lives. Yet, because we live in a mobile society and have so many choices, the individual child's quest for meaning is no small challenge. Belonging and having clarity about identity—once built into life—must today be discovered, articulated, and chosen. Parents must help their children as they grow to meet these less tangible, moral needs. Do we teach our children to appreciate not only the obvious value of material goods, but also the gifts of the Spirit? Do we recognize the role we play in helping them discover and acknowledge a purpose and meaning in their lives? When the candy of material goods ceases to satisfy them, where will they turn?

It is natural to determine success, in part, in economic terms. However, more is needed if we desire our children's full development. A term borrowed from game theory—*zero-sum game*—may be helpful in understanding why a narrow focus on economic success, to the exclusion of broader human success, is ultimately harmful: In a world of diminishing resources and power imbalance, nations compete for control over all kinds of resources. Some nations have a fear of "running out." Their drive to compete and accumulate material resources and capital assumes that when one nation is winning, the others must lose by an equal amount—together this adds up to a *zero-sum*. Competitive striving in an unfriendly environment is the world-view of the zero-sum-game theorists. They don't advocate for such a world. They simply believe these are the facts: scarcity, division, competition, and diminishing returns.

One of the side effects of living in a culture affected by a zero-sum-game worldview is aggressive behavior. Aggression is fueled by a desire to secure optimal benefits for oneself to the exclusion of others. Other kinds of behavior—like cheating, lying, and refusing to respect others—can be rationalized in the context of self-preservation in a competitive zero-sum world.

The gospel calls families to live in a way totally antithetical to this. Bonnie Miller-McLemore points out the connection between our love for our own children and the care of all God's children:

> The Christian tradition asks us to generalize our intense love of our closest family members to include our farthest and most marginalized neighbors. With my children, something propels me at times to extend myself at greater cost and to a greater extent than I might once have thought possible. It is precisely this impulse of self-extension for our most proximate loved ones...that Christianity has commanded us to extend to our neighbors at large. We are to build on such passion, not reject it.[2]

The act of parenting teaches us that we have abundant love to give. To assume that when one of our children wins, the other loses would be preposterous. On the contrary, healthy families strive to love each child equally and not favor one over the other. While we often show our love in giving material things, love still transcends the gift it accompanies. The dynamic of abundant love replaces the zero-sum game. When we love each of our children and help each to thrive in his or her way, we emulate God's love for humanity, a love that is a universal, timeless embrace extended to all without discrimination.

Of course, every family experiences normal competitive behavior, jealousy, and other strife between siblings. Yet the general rule remains love. What binds us together for the sake of survival is rooted in this love. Yet God calls us to stretch this love among ourselves and to share, with faith in the abundance of love, beyond our family circle. As we care for our own, our hearts can be opened to more fully love others, for to love our own children is to begin to love all God's children. Parenting widens our embrace.

Ours is a time when this widening embrace can flower. Sophisticated and rapid communication of different kinds makes us aware of suffering, abuse, poverty, epidemics, natural disasters, crime, and other social ills. Yet, are we not also made aware of the many men and women working to restore human dignity by pursuing education and development? While in daily life we may not be in contact with the people involved, our knowledge alone widens our circle of those we can call our neighbors.

Is it not an undue burden to be aware of the need and suffering around us? Consider, for a moment, that the opposite is true. When Blessed Teresa of Calcutta received the Nobel Peace Prize, she was asked what people could do to work for peace. She said, "Go home and love your families." For her, peace was built from the inside out, beginning with respect and love toward our own, in our home and with our neighbors around us. How we live with each other in concrete daily interactions is the means of collaborating with God in redeeming a lost and weary world. We may feel the burden of resisting loving others, because we are too busy and too engrossed in other things. Yet, as our own family continues to challenge us to do the work of love, our hearts can be enlarged to love even more, to love in abundance!

In feeding *this* need, the need others have of us, we and our children can grow in a sense of meaning and purpose—the very thing we lack! Mother Teresa of Calcutta encouraged her sisters to practice plain, ordinary thoughtfulness. It was the beginning of great sanctity. She also believed in the power of joy, yet insisted it wasn't enough to smile. You had to smile without discrimination, to offer your joy to people you didn't know or even like. This was the means of building peace, to *practice* seeing others as part of God's family and treating them this way.[3]

We live in such a state of constant cynicism that we may feel unable to imagine the beauty of God and creation shining through the hurtful things of the world. Let us pause to remember that God expects us to hope and work toward peace, toward a more just treatment of each person, and toward a more just system. Things could be different, *should* be different. This requires that we renounce the cultural norm of seeing the world as a diminishing resource in a zero-sum game. What difference would it make to see the children of others with a kind of familial love? What economic and social needs might diminish and even be slowly overcome? We will have saved our own lives in the process.

2. The Oil That Never Runs Dry: God's Abundance

In the practical-minded culture we inhabit 24/7, such notions as extending familial love may seem undesirable. We barely have time to tend to our own lives. How can we possibly make room for others? Yet Scripture shows us God's promise of abundance. The story of the widow of Zarephath demonstrates this.

During the time of the prophet Elijah, a great famine comes to the land of Israel, caused by drought. There is no rain for three-and-a-half years. A Gentile widow is starving. One morning, she is out collecting firewood to prepare some food for herself and her son. She has only a few drops of oil and just enough meal to make a few small cakes of bread to eat. With her food stores depleted and her heart without hope, she expects to die. At this low ebb of her life, God sends her the prophet Elijah. Does he offer to save her? No. He asks her for water and a "morsel" of bread!

They look at each other, the mother and the man of God. Each is confronted by death, each striving to hang on to life through a bit of bread. The "mother bear" rises in her as she looks at him and worries about her son.

She tells Elijah that she's about to prepare a cake with the last bit of meal in the house and the last drop of oil. She and her son will eat it and then die. The prophet tells her, "Do not be afraid," and then instructs her to prepare food for him first, then for her family. "For thus says the LORD, the God of Israel: The jar of meal will not be emptied and the jug of oil will not fail until the day that the LORD sends rain on the earth" (1 Kings 17:13–14).

The widow believes Elijah's promise and does as the prophet asks her. His word comes to pass: The oil does not run dry; the meal keeps appearing in the bottom of her jar. The widow and her son survive the famine, because she trusted the Word of God spoken by the prophet.

I saw this kind of faith in God's providence everywhere in postwar Guatemala. I saw it in the children who valued a blessing with oil, and in the religious processions of Palm Sunday, when the people took to the streets to hail Jesus as their King— an overt sign of defiance to the government. These were the ways they asserted God's power, as if to say, "Don't you know? God will protect us in our extreme vulnerability. This is something we can hold on to. We will not give it up or settle for less than God as our protector."

How do we live out God's abundance in our own family? The prophet did not just happen to find the widow, but was sent specifically to her (1 Kings 17:8). Families who believe are sent to notice the poor in order to take part of God's provision for others. Abundance can appear in the midst of poverty when someone listens in compassion and shares—even out of scarcity.

There is a mutual exchange in the Old Testament story: The poor widow first gives a gift of water and bread. Then she receives. As in the gospel story of the multiplication of the loaves and the fishes, a modest gift of a few loaves and fishes is presented first. Then the crowd of five thousand can be fed out of God's abundance. There is a need for interpersonal giving and receiving on both sides. The gift of the widow is necessary too. So the poor share their faith and enrich those who would reach out to them. Only then is the promise of God's hidden abundance made manifest.

Poverty can be a sign of God's kingdom only when those who experience it depend on God and when those who see it recognize a duty to respond. The "kingdom" is not of this world, so the rules of our human systems do not govern this reality. The kingdom is at the same time a destination and a reality already begun in our midst.

For many of us, the kingdom of God or the reign of God conjures up a strange image of crowns and thrones. As a scriptural term, however, it is a key metaphor Jesus uses to describe an indescribable reality: the Spirit of God ruling the heart of every person. This reign is near to us, but is also something we can squander or ultimately lose (Matt 10:7 and 7:21); it requires that we repent in action, not simply in word, and that we become like children (Matt 3:2, 7:21, 18:3). It is difficult to enter for those who are "rich" to enter the kingdom, but "all things are possible" with God (Matt 19:23ff). Jesus uses parables to hint at God's reign; it is like a merchant looking for pearls (Matt 13:44–46) or a king who throws a wedding banquet for his son (Matt 2:22). It belongs to the humble, those persecuted for righteousness, the poor in spirit, and those who do the will of the Father in heaven (Matt 18:4, 5:10, 5:3, 7:21). It is likened to a kingdom only to demonstrate that power in human affairs is at stake, but this power is not bound by any earthly political organization (John 18:36). Rather, it is likened to a kind of energy, like the zeal of a man driven to search for a treasure, or the tender love of a father filled with joy for his son who is young and in love. The reign of God is free, but it is also elusive and costly.

Oil is an ancient symbol of royalty. It is featured in Scripture as a symbol of Jesus' kingship. At baptism, we are anointed with oil as a sign of becoming part of the family of God through Jesus, so that we share in an abundant inheritance in Jesus. Possessing the kingdom of God does not depend on secret knowledge or on being better than anyone else: it is neither gnostic nor elitist. It depends solely on the right to inherit the reign of God because of faith in Jesus. When we possess it, the kingdom frees us from the laws of miserly grasping that rule the kingdoms of this world, which pass.

The works of parenting embody the works of the kingdom. They include all the corporal works of mercy: feeding the hungry, clothing the naked, and tending the sick, to name a few. They also include the spiritual works of mercy: comforting the afflicted, teaching the ignorant, giving counsel, and so forth. Faith always challenges us to open our hearts more: to see others inclusively, called to God's royal family as well.

Elijah told the widow not to be afraid. It is often fear that prevents us from taking action, especially as mothers and parents. We don't want those we love to suffer because of our decisions. Elijah respects the widow's fear and reassures her. When she decides to trust him, her faith and her just action become the means of her and her son's salvation.

3. Community: Mothers from Every Nation, Tribe, and Tongue

In the life parable related at the start of this chapter, the words *You are one of us*, spoken by our Guatemalan guide, struck me deeply. I was not one of them! Yet when he said this, I knew he was right. The words seemed true despite all the evidence that my rational mind offered to the contrary. What, then, allowed me to be one of them that afternoon, even if for a fleeting few minutes?

The secret seemed to lie in the interaction I had with the children: First we ran out of something—candy. Then the oil filled in the gap with God's abundance. What happened next was of the Spirit, who gave us understanding and joy in each other's presence. It was the Spirit among us that allowed me to be one of them. God filled our shared human scarcity, and we simply rejoiced over God's provision.

A similar dynamic, a similar movement of the Spirit, can happen in various situations where people reach out to each other from vastly different starting places. For example, during natural disasters, people can come together and exhibit heroic efforts to help those affected, even though they are usually strangers. Yet such things are part of daily life as well. We as women participate in the dynamic of the Spirit when we turn to each other and lean on each other for help as new mothers. At these times too our differences seem to fade in importance.

The bonds between women are a key aspect of motherhood. Seeking each other's help, we are kept sane by wisdom and company, and this can add greatly to our happiness as mothers. Through these bonds we learn to mother ourselves. This fellowship is also extended to our families. It is often women who come together and then invite men and children to share community. In this way, all can be immersed in the waters of human connectedness. Although we may have ignored this connectedness before, we can't afford to miss now! We find ourselves associating with all kinds of families, and not necessarily people we would choose: they are the ones who happen to be having babies when we are, or signing up for soccer, or enrolling at a university. Jesus compared the kingdom of heaven to a great net that is cast into the sea and brings up many fish (Matt 13:47). So, children bring together the diverse family of God, pushing us into close proximity with one another and breathing into us the life of community. This enriches us beyond measure. It causes us to stretch continually in seeing others as related, as family, and to rejoice in the beauty of the sheer variety of families.

Naturally, friendship is based on taste and preferences, but the community that arises out of this jumble of people experiencing parenthood together goes beyond just choice. We may think community is the coming together of like-minded people. It can be this, but the Christian sense of community is Pentecost: the coming together of people who are different. The Spirit fosters a natural human potential to imagine what it would be like to be in the situation of another person, and so creates empathy, compassion, patience, respect, and mercy. God helps us imagine and respect that difference by direct contact. We learn to listen

to and honor the experience of others, person by person, and
break out of our prejudices toward one another. As at Pentecost,
the Spirit can help us understand each other, "each in his own
tongue" (Acts 2:6–12).

In God's family, diversity is not just "slapped on," as if to
fill a quota. Christian communion is essentially diverse. Hence
the metaphor of St. Paul: the Church is a body, with different
parts, each having its own function, its own glory and honor, its
own place in the working together of the whole, with God as its
head. The Church could not function were it not diverse. Some
have called ours the Age of the Spirit and this is an apt description, for modern minds and hearts long for something greater
than our immediate concerns. The reality of life's diversity can
challenge us to seek out and embrace that which transcends and
therefore unites us.

Motherhood is an opportunity to experience this transcendence firsthand. It can break us open and prepare our hearts to
love without discrimination, awakening a potential to love
beyond anything we had known before. Through mothering
itself, God asks us to collaborate in the divine work: the
fatherly-motherly love of the Creator, and the restorative love of
the Spirit who restores all things in Jesus. As we love and serve
within our families, as we minister to each child, with his or her
own personality, amid struggles and through our human failing
and sin, we become living signs of God's indiscriminate love. We
participate in that love in the most concrete, incarnational way.
And through this love, we also benefit society.

Mothers too-easily discount the value of this humble work.
We don't rightly know the gift our children can be to the world.
Inspired by the words of former president John F. Kennedy, we
can say: Ask not what the world can do for my child, but what
my child might one day do for the world. One person can do
great good or great ill, and we contribute to the future world by
bringing up our child as we do.

Living in harmony with diversity involves a leap, a leap out
of self, toward the other. To do this, we have to overcome our
fear and trust God to provide. The Spirit summons us from
within to do the works of love that heal us from division. It uni-

fies us and makes us shine like the city on a hill, like the diamond, the pearl, like the lamp giving light to all around us. True and lasting community takes us into God and creates us anew into an inseparable family of love.

THE CHANGING FACE OF MOTHERHOOD

Motherhood has changed because women have changed. Responding to the changes that come with modernity, women have had to evaluate and reevaluate work, family, even the very meaning of being a woman. We continue on that road of discovery. Some of those adjustments include an ideal of love that has become an essential aspect of marriage and the value of autonomy to pursue interests outside our familial commitments. We know how crucial economic independence can be. As mothers, we also have new attitudes toward raising our children that are more open. We see ourselves as midwives to our children's fuller development, helping them search for and fulfill their own hopes and dreams. We experience family life as mobile and expect our children to have more opportunities. Children are no longer considered the possessions of their fathers: we as mothers have increasing say in their fate.

Cultural shifts in women's identity have an impact on the family and therefore on society. This is especially true when women have taken action for the sake of their children's well-being and of the communities where they live.

Mothers have more voice today, and that voice will grow in influence. Women effect social change when that change is necessary for the good of their children. In the past, mothers have organized to demand laws against child labor and drunk driving. Today, women in war-torn countries fight, often putting their lives in grave peril, to bring basic development to their communities. They see their young sons carrying guns, with no jobs and too much time on their hands. It is women and mothers who are stepping into the breach left by decades-long conflicts all over the world and also asking for collaboration from those who have already won these battles. Their voices are being heard today more than ever. Tortured by war and by the rape of their bodies and the land, mothers have begun to stand up to war and say, "No more." These women's stories are shared and spread.

For this reason, women—like the Iraqi Zainab Salabi, who founded Women for Women International—go into the most dangerous places on earth to meet with other women and assist them in turning their lives and communities around. They link with others who support their work, fund businesses, and even pair women with companions in the West who commit to help support them in developing their work and in furthering the health of their families. This is a profound challenge to the violence that persists at the heart of human sinfulness.

The face of motherhood today is more resolute. It is the face of a woman standing against the devaluation of human life. There is hope and determination on that face and, most of all, a sense of possibility and joy that, as women collaborate to challenge forces that conspire to harm their children, they can build the reign of God. This is what has us headed down the road to peace. This peace is the greatest gift we can bequeath our children.

ENCOUNTER AND PRACTICE

Encounter

In the small Guatemalan villages I visited, women would not allow me to photograph them. Children, however, were a different story. As the women shielded their own faces and even growled at me whenever I approached with my camera, they pushed their children forward. The children loved to be photographed; they smiled and whirled in front of the lens. Small boys sat in doorways and little girls carried siblings only slightly smaller than themselves. Children were these people's greatest riches.

1. *You Are Precious to God.* Settle yourself for meditation as usual (find your quiet place, practice breathing, and so on). Remember a joyful day from

your childhood. Imagine God near you, proud of you: encouraging you forward to live your life to the fullest, calling you to work, putting faith in you, in the dreams of your life being realized. Can you imagine God calling you by name, saying, "You are my son or daughter, in whom I am well pleased"(Matt 3:17)?

2. *Your Child Is Precious to God.* Alternate meditation: Imagine your child (one at a time, if you have several) at different stages of his or her life. Give thanks for the gift of that particular child and for his or her gifts. You may draw on a psalm verse to pray for your child, blessing his or her future, giving thanks for the graces of the past God has already given. Can you see God calling your son or daughter, saying, "You are my child in whom I am well pleased"?

3. *What Is Your Treasure?* What do you consider your most prized possession? It might be a keepsake or a picture, or perhaps something one of your children made for you. How might this object symbolize the kingdom of God for you? Notice when you see examples of your prized possession as you go through your day. Ask God to teach you about the kingdom of heaven through this symbol.

Practice

1. *Discover and Write Your Own Life Parable.* The life of the Spirit is close to us, all around us and in us. Sometimes we become aware of it breaking through, unexpectedly, refreshingly, to give us a new perspective. At these moments, grace may enable us to see something we didn't notice before, right there in what we see, hear, touch, smell, and taste, but with *further* intensity. Like radio signals, the Holy Spirit sends out signals to anyone able to

listen, sends out "broadcasts" of the reign of God to anyone with ears to hear.

Imagine Jesus inviting you to become more aware of the work of God in the world and asking you to build the reign of God among us. Choose an event in your life, some memory that has special meaning for you. It may be an experience you have often reflected on, or one that has only just begun to hold meaning for you. Ponder this memory over the next week. Write it down in story form or prose. How has God touched you through this memory, your life parable?

2. *Love the One in Front of You.* The saints were the most human among us, yet the most alive with the desire for God. That desire compelled them toward greater charity. Our daily limitations and failures may sometimes make us feel powerless, but by our attention and love for the person right in front of us, we are put in immediate contact with the grace of the kingdom of God.

Make a list of the people you interact with on a given day: co-workers, your husband or wife, your children, the children of other people, friends, siblings, parents, strangers, service workers, and so on. Practice being fully present to one person and notice how you interact with him or her. Write a description of your routine way of treating him or her. What do you love about it? What would you change? On another day, choose someone else. Try to build a habit of practicing reign of God with whomever you find in front of you today.

The Mother's Calling

Love in the Heart of the World

New mothers go into a cave. When they look out on the world again, they forever look at it differently. Our domesticity is short-lived, especially in today's world. When we look out the front door, we are reminded that the baby we have nestled into sleep and nursed to contentment will also one day walk out that door. We have an immeasurable stake in the state of the world that our children will face as they toddle, walk, and then stride out that door. Historically, mothers have recognized they have a part to play in shaping and forming the world, and some have paid dearly for their efforts.

Ours is a special time of opportunity to try something new, to look for ways of living that foster simplicity, community, and the common good. We may be afraid to share what we have when we imagine there is a chance that handing out our bread will leave our own children hungry. Yet this is precisely what is needed to protect our own children in the long term. There are many families who don't have the luxury of choosing to get along with less. Our efforts, however small, have great potential to feed the spiritual longings that haunt us. These longings conspire to free us from the treadmill of overconsumption. Poverty of spirit works to gradually untie our bonds. It frees us to take the hand of other people in need.

There is a story that Mother Teresa of Calcutta frequently told. She was on the street in London and noticed a man who was very intoxicated. His face was etched with deep sadness and loneliness. She approached the man, wondering what he must be feeling. Taking his hands in her own, she asked him simply, "How are you today?" He looked up at her and exclaimed, "Oh! Finally the warmth of someone's hands touching mine!" and his face was transformed into a delighted smile. According to Mother Teresa, this kind of action, something any one of us could do, would lead to peace in our times. These gestures may seem small, but as Mother Teresa and others continue to show, we cannot achieve the bigger peace without this daily, humble, small peace. To repeat: When she won the Nobel Peace Prize, Mother Teresa was asked, "What can we do to further peace?" She answered simply, "Go home and love your families." That love—learned in and spread beyond the home—is God's way of saving humanity. It is not only experts, theologians, or mystics who do this work, but lovers of humanity, wherever they are found.

At the end of life, we will be judged on love. In the Gospel of Matthew, Jesus provided all the answers to the test of the last judgment. He said to those he was inviting into heaven : "Come, you that are blessed by my Father,...for I was hungry and you gave me food, I was thirsty and you gave me something to drink....Come...inherit the kingdom" (Matt 25:34–35, 34).

Notes

CHAPTER ONE: YOU ARE CHOSEN

1. Walter A. Elwell, ed., *Baker Topical Guide to the Bible* (Grand Rapids: Baker Books, 1991), 476–77.

2. Ellyn Sanna, *Motherhood: A Spiritual Journey* (New York / Mahwah, NJ: Paulist Press, 1997), 12.

3. Ibid.

4. Bonnie J. Miller-McLemore, *In the Midst of Chaos: Caring for Children as Spiritual Practice* (San Francisco: Jossey-Bass, 2007), 95–96.

5. Donald E. Gowan, ed., *The Westminster Theological Wordbook of the Bible* (Louisville, KY: Westminster John Knox Press, 2003), 53–55.

6. Miller-McLemore, 24–25.

7. Ann Tremaine Linthorst, *Mothering as a Spiritual Journey* (New York: Crossroad, 1998), 21.

8. Sanna, 103.

9. Ibid., 101.

10. Ibid., 102.

11. Miller-McLemore, xvi.

12. Linthorst, 32–34.

13. Jess Stern, ed., *The Random House College Dictionary: Revised Edition* (New York: Random House, Inc., 1988), 974.

CHAPTER TWO:
BE FRUITFUL AND MULTIPLY

1. Sanna, 18. See also Trudelle Thomas, *Spirituality in the Mother Zone: Staying Centered, Finding God* (New York / Mahwah, NJ: Paulist Press, 2005), 51–52.

2. Augustine, *Confessions*, Betty Radice, ed., R. S. Pine-Coffin, tr. (Harmondsworth, Middlesex, England: Penguin Classics, 1961), Book 1:1.

3. Rev. William Saunders, "What are the 'O Antiphons'?" from the Catholic Education Resource Center at *www.catholic education.org/articles/religion/re0374.html.*

4. Joseph Rickaby, *The Spiritual Exercises of St. Ignatius of Loyola: Spanish and English* (London: Burns and Oats, Limited, 1915), no. 48, my trans.

5. Joseph Tetlow, *Choosing Christ in the World: Directing the Spiritual Exercises of St. Ignatius of Loyola According to Annotations Eighteen and Nineteen: A Handbook* (St. Louis: Institute of Jesuit Sources, 1989), 202.

6. Ibid.

7. This does not refer to predestination, a concept that is not believed by the Catholic Church. Catholic tradition points to God's omniscience and humanity's free will as a mystery; that is, God can know us, know the whole of our lives in their complexity, and yet does not manipulate our freedom.

8. The distinction should be made between quality and quantity. It is possible to spend entire days with our children and never engage them because we are distracted or too fatigued to really pay attention to them. Quality of attention is what I want to emphasize.

9. Pam England and Rob Horowitz, *Birthing From Within: an Extra-Ordinary Guide to Childbirth Preparation* (Albuquerque, NM: Partera Press, 1998), Introduction, xv.

10. Ibid., 32.

11. Ibid., quotations at 176 and 9.

12. Ibid., 8–9.

13. Sanna, 53–54.

CHAPTER THREE: LOVE AS YOU ARE LOVED

1. Wendy Wright, *Seasons of a Family's Life: Cultivating the Contemplative Spirit at Home* (San Francisco: Jossey-Bass, 2003), 11.

2. Ibid., 16.

3. Susan J. Douglas and Meredith W. Michaels, *The Mommy Myth: The Idealization of Motherhood and How It Has Undermined Women* (New York: Free Press, 2004), 26.

4. Marjorie Spruill Wheeler, ed., *One Woman, One Vote: Rediscovering the Woman Suffrage Movement* (Troutdale, OR: NewSage Press, 1995), 117–33.

5. Jess Stein, ed., *The Random House College Dictionary Revised Edition* (New York: Random House, 1988), 913.

6. Sara Ruddick, quoted in Carol Lee Flinders, *Enduring Grace: Living Portraits of Seven Women Mystics* (San Francisco: HarperSanFrancisco, 1993), 8.

7. Wright, 16.

8. Jim Fay and Charles Fay, *Love and Logic Magic for Early Childhood: Practical Parenting from Birth to Six Years* (Golden, CO: The Love and Logic Press, Inc., 2000). My understanding of empathetic responses in parenting is based on the approach recommended by these authors.

9. Denise Roy, *My Monastery Is a Minivan: Where the Daily Is Divine and the Routine Becomes Prayer* (Chicago: Loyola Press, 2001), 88.

10. Wright, 22.

11. Flinders, 13.

12. M. L. del Mastro, trans., *The Revelation of Divine Love in Sixteen Showings Made to Dame Julian of Norwich* (Liguori, MO: Liguori/Triumph, 1994), 168–69.

13. Sarah McElwain, ed., *Saying Grace: Blessings for the Family Table* (San Francisco: Chronicle Books, 2003), 74.

CHAPTER FOUR: DO NOT BE AFRAID

1. Christine Northrup, MD, *Women's Bodies, Women's Wisdom: Creating Physical and Emotional Health and Healing* (New York: Bantam Books, 1994), 525.

2. Sanna, 5.

3. Wright, 110.

4. Aschenbrenner, 5.

5. Wright, 112.

6. Ibid., 116.

CHAPTER FIVE: FILLED WITH COMPASSION

1. Kate Figes and Jean Zimmerman, *Life After Birth: What Even Your Friends Won't Tell You about Motherhood* (New York: St. Martin's Press, 1998), 164.

2. Ibid., 166.

3. Joan Chittister, *In the Heart of the Temple: My Spiritual Vision for Today's World* (New York: BlueBridge, 2004), 51.

4. For an excellent discussion on the role of language used in Scripture to portray God, see Sandra M. Schneiders, *Women and the Word: The Gender of God in the New Testament and the Spirituality of Women* (New York: Paulist Press, 1986), esp. 20–37.

5. The reality of sin would not exist if not for the fact that God creates human life to be free, with will and reason, in "God's image."

6. Chittister, 45.

CHAPTER SIX: BLESSED ARE YOU

1. W. E. Vine, *Vine's Expository Dictionary* (Nashville: Nelson Thomas Publishers, 1997), 125.

2. John Trent and Gary Smalley, *The Blessing: Giving the Gift of Unconditional Love and Acceptance* (Nashville: Nelson Books, 1993), 32.

3. *Random House College Dictionary*, 1287–288.

4. Trent and Smalley, 30.

5. David G. Benner, *The Gift of Being Yourself: The Sacred Call to Self-Discovery* (Downers Grove, IL: InterVarsity Press, 2004), 61.

6. Trent and Smalley, 42.

7. Ibid., 133–35.

8. Ibid., 31.

9. Personality differences have a role in how feelings are felt and communicated. Classic personality definitions outlined in systems like Myers-Briggs and the Enneagram can help clarify how individuals experience emotion differently. For example, a person who is identified as more of a thinker on the Enneagram system may experience quieter emotions than someone else. In order to say, "I love you," in earnest, such a person does not have to feel overwhelmed with fervor. The word still carries the power to communicate love to the recipient.

10. See Trent and Smalley, 76, on the difficulty of expressing love.

11. Ibid., 107.

12. Ibid., 121 ff.

13. Ibid., 39.

CHAPTER SEVEN: COME INHERIT THE KINGDOM

1. Miller-McLemore, 103.

2. Ibid., 113.

3. Michael Collopy, *Works of Love Are Works of Peace: Mother Teresa of Calcutta and the Missionaries of Charity* (San Francisco: Ignatius Press, 1996), throughout.